Lawless Wealth

Lawless Wealth

The Origin of Some
Great American Fortunes

CHARLES EDWARD RUSSELL

COSIMOCLASSICS

NEW YORK

Lawless Wealth: The Origin of Some Great American Fortunes
Originally published in 1908 by B. W. Dodge & Company, New York
This edition published by Cosimo Classics in 2023

Cover copyright © 2023 by Cosimo, Inc.
Cover design by www.heatherkern.com
Cover image, cartoon, "Our robber barons" in *Puck Magazine* by Bernhard Gillam, 1882.
Sourced from Wikimedia Commons:
https://commons.wikimedia.org/wiki/File:Our_robber_barons_-_Gillam._LCCN2012647214.jpg

ISBN: 978-1-64679-883-4

This edition is a replica of a rare classic. As such, it is possible that some of the text might be blurred or of reduced print quality. Thank you for your understanding, and we wish you a pleasant reading experience.

Ordering Information:
Cosimo publications are available at online bookstores. They may also be purchased for educational, business, or promotional use:
    Bulk orders: Special discounts are available on bulk orders for reading groups, organizations, businesses, and others.
    Custom-label orders: We offer selected books with your customized cover or logo of choice.

For more information, contact us at www.cosimobooks.com

CONTENTS

vi   *CONTENTS*

THE land of England has ruled it for six hundred years. The corporations of America mean to rule it in the same way, and, unless some power more radical than that of ordinary politics is found, will rule it inevitably. I confess that the only fear I have in regard to republican institutions is whether, in our day, any adequate remedy will be found for this widening flood of the power of incorporated wealth.

—*Wendell Phillips.*

LAWLESS WEALTH

CHAPTER I

GOLDEN TIDES ABOUT THE GOLDEN CITY

HERE, at the gateway of a world, sits the imperial city of New York, and about her and over her is piled such wealth as men have never before dreamed of.

How wonderful it all is! Daily in this richest of cities you can see the golden flood rising and never ebbing. So much wealth, so much luxury, such a bewildering display, such a concentration of the power for which money is only a symbol has not been known in the records of the race. No other men have been so rich as some New York men; so many rich men have not gathered in another place. With pride and awe we count here one man whose wealth is reputed to be one thousand million dollars, five men whose wealth is estimated at more than three hundred millions each, ten men whose wealth is reported to be one hundred millions each, four thousand men whose wealth is computed at one million or more each.   In face of these stupendous totals the mind staggers and hardly apprehends the significance of the figures; but everywhere the eye can see the physical and enduring monuments of existing conditions.   Those strange gigantic structures, massed one upon another, mile after mile, in the business region—in all the world where can you find an equal expression of power and energy?   And the palaces grouped about the park—how plainly they speak of the ceaseless tide of gold that sweeps into this unique habitat of men!

No, not elsewhere can you find such wealth; in few places such tremendous and thought-compelling contrasts.   How strange to go from upper Fifth Avenue and stand before that block in Orchard Street that is the most densely populated spot on this earth!   The utmost extremes of attainable magnificence and endurable misery seem bent around to touch within this marvelous city.

If the figures and analyses of the sociologists hold true, here are 10,000 persons that are rich, 500,000 that are well-to-do, 1,500,000 that are poor,

2,000,000 that are very poor. Take, then, these
3,500,000 of the poor and very poor. How comes
it that the golden flood misses them? Here it runs
all about them, so deep and wide a current that the
imperial city wantons in it and wastes it and plays
with it. And here are 2,000,000 that seem to
have little or none of it. Why so little? Or why
none? The fact is apparent enough. Do but
walk through the district east of the Bowery and
Third Avenue and south of Twenty-third Street;
you shall have evidence convincing. Go into some
of the courts and rear tenements in the region, let
us say, between the two bridge terminals. The
filthy and vilely overcrowded dwellings, the pois-
oned air, the moldy dampness of ancient and dark
passageways, the reeking halls, the malarial areas,
the ragged crowds, the toiling men, the tired
women, the ill-developed, half-nourished children,
the jostling masses on the sidewalks, the forlorn
and unkempt appearance of the streets, the painful
evidences of a daily and grim struggle, hand-to-
hand, eye-to-eye, for bare life and breath, the
women thrust into unwomanly employments, the
children at work when they should be at school—
you know all these things well if you have ever
strayed into that noisome territory. Plainly, no

golden flood touches these sodden and unclean shores.

And how is it with the 1,500,000 of the next above stratum, upon whom is laid a need only less harsh? In thousands of modest flats in the better regions dwell these families that win larger incomes, the families of the employed men, the clerks, the salesmen, the regulars and non-commissioned officers in the army of industry. The average wealth among these, we are told, is $1,639. How far that bears us from the plashings of the golden stream! The furniture in the little flat and the savings of the good man and the economies of the wife, and all they have together, to wear and to use and to bequeath, are worth $1,639. He has an annual salary, perhaps $2,000, the good man. From that in a city where the cost of living is greater than in any other city of men, he must feed and clothe the family, pay his rent (which shows steadily a tendency to increase), maintain his life insurance, if he be prudent, and lay by for the day when he shall be no longer able to earn. And his rent alone is one-fourth or more of his income. How does life go in that little flat? From where he stands and toils, if he looks up to no more than a ledge of security, the distance seems impossible;

up to a competence, overwhelming; to wealth, a mere dream. Yet men have traversed it; he knows that. By what incomprehensible genius, by what great gifts of mind wholly distinguishing them from other men, by what totally differing structure of brain cells have they achieved it?

He knows that in his country opportunity must be for all men equal. Often he heard it declared to be thus equal when he was a boy and went to Fourth of July meetings in the country; often he has read the same statement since. So that the trouble with him is in himself. Clearly he lacks the mental capacity to be rich.

And he finds that this is the opinion of the world also. He finds that in the opinion of mankind the inequality between his state and the state of the 10,000, and the still more terrible contrast between the 10,000 and the 2,000,000 are perfectly explained, perfectly justified, perfectly established, as eternally right, reasonable and moral, by this difference in brain cells.

Moreover, he learns that there is another reason. The men that are deepest in the stream are, by common report, further endowed than with merely this rare wondrous gift of ability. They have done something. These are the men upon whom rest

the foundations of prosperity. They say so.
Others say so. The world seems to accept and
believe the doctrine as a thing not to be ques-
tioned. The newspapers chronicle respectfully the
doing and the sayings of these men; reflections or
adverse comments upon them are resented as con-
stituting assaults upon the bases of the general welfare. Like an inverted pyramid, the 500,000, the
1,500,000 and the 2,000,000 repose upon the
things done by the 10,000. In a way almost sacred
the 10,000 seem to hold the palladium of national
progress. Thus, by the gift of this ability that
so sets them apart and marks them from other men,
they, according to the entertained theory, have developed the railroads, built the factories, established the commerce, created the industries of the
land. Upon these railroads, factories, commerce,
industries, depend the employment and conse-
quently the lives of the 1,500,000 that have little
ability and of the 2,000,000 that have none.
Therefore, on all grounds of the strictest moral
principle, the 10,000 that are blessed with ability
are entitled to all else they have possessed themselves of.

I am a plain man from the West, and I have in
the golden imperial city a friend among the 1,500,-

ooo of the little able, and he takes me forth to view the wonders of the vast human hive about us. We see very many things that instruct my ungifted mind. We traverse these miles of gigantic buildings, and I glimpse a little of the incalculable, indomitable, abnormal force that they represent; and then he takes me to view the region where dwell the 4,000 men that control this force.

It is all very wonderful. The great white gleaming palaces remind me of the pictures I have seen of stately structures in European capitals. Here is a house with a broad driveway sweeping clear to the front door and with no other exit, as if the inmates never walk when they go abroad. Under a kind of beautiful canopy, all glass and bronze-like metal, a carriage is waiting, a great shining chariot, with much silver and crystal, very handsome. The driver has a sort of uniform with a dark green coat and very big silver buttons and a high silk hat with something on it and very white trousers that look as if they were made of some kind of white leather, and high boots with yellow tops; and by the carriage door is another man dressed exactly like the driver. How stately and impressive is the show!

We pass another house, very large and commanding, with a little patch of ground about it and a very high steel fence on all sides.   We pass other magnificent houses, stone, of an even brown color, very pleasing; enormous houses of a solid and serious architecture.   Then we come to large and beautiful buildings that are pointed out to me as the homes of different clubs of successful men; and again to many others, almost or quite as large, that are merely residences.   I see innumerable automobiles; everybody in this smiling and prosperous region seems to have an automobile.   I am told that many of the residents have a dozen automobiles apiece, different styles for different occasions; one automobile to shop in, and one to use in the park, and one to use in the country, and one for a few persons, and one for six or eight; large automobiles and small automobiles for different purposes and humors, with expert servants to operate them quickly and safely and transform the task of travel into a sensuous delight.   With joy I hear of these things: to my mind they illustrate progress.)

There are no cheap nor mean nor repulsive-looking houses here, nor ill-fed people, no stuffy courts, no malodorous hallways; but all things betoken comfort and prosperity.   The sidewalks are never crowded, there is plenty of air and sunlight, the

people are always well dressed and look gentle and
happy.   The sun shines and the rows of palaces
gleam in the keen light.   Across the street is the
park and that is beautiful too: the white houses
make an agreeable contrast against all that mass of
vivid green.   I look at the whole extraordinary
spectacle, and it seems to me typical of the wealth
and the peculiar greatness of my country.

For, say I to myself, here is the very summit of
opportunity, here is the crowning triumph of the
principle of a free field to all, this shows what men
can do when, unhampered by the foolish govern-
mental interference of the older world, they are
set down before the opened gates of fortune.   The
men that built all these beautiful houses, say I to
myself, were the gifted generals on the commercial
battlefield, and their dwellings are emblematical of
their victories, as of old time men used to win suits
of armor in the tourney.   Doubtless, I say, in the
first house lives a great merchant.   By his ability,
energy, and foresight he built a great business, he
brought together producer and consumer, he established a great mart, he supplied a want of society.
By the rules of the war game and of our civilization
this is his reward.

And the next house belongs to a man that developed the railroad service of the United States; he built new lines and improved old. By his ability, energy, and foresight he made transportation cheap and easy. He served society well, and by the rules of the war game this is his reward.

And the next house is the house of a man that developed the coal industry. He improved and cheapened coal production, he made fuel cheaper in the world, he lessened the burden of the ungifted. By his ability, energy and foresight he built a great and useful business; he served society well, and by the rules of the war game this is his reward.

And the next house is the house of a man that developed a great manufacturing enterprise. By his ability, energy and foresight he constructed a system whereby something should be supplied that all men needed—shoes, perhaps, or hats. He made these things cheap and plentiful for all mankind, he was of use to society, and this is his reward.

With pleasure I reflect upon all these things: they prove again the greatness of my country and again the triumph of that free opportunity of which we have ever been proud. True, I cannot see exactly wherein my ungifted friend at my side has much share in this glorious opportunity. True, it appears certain that all his life he will struggle dubiously for each day's bread and be pursued by the specters of rent and butchers' bills. True, I have a disagreeable reflection that fuel has not been made cheaper in the world, that production has not been furthered, that the essential state of the overwhelming majority of mankind has not been notably improved. True, we have journeyed uptown by way of Attorney Street and Columbia Street and Avenue B, and while I rejoice at the scene now before me, there is a memory I could well spare of scenes lately passed, and a traitorous suggestion that the rewards are disproportionate. But undeniably they are admirable and rich, as here they appear massed before me, and that is the true American way, to give with liberal hand. Indeed, how typically American it all is! These men were the free architects of their own fortunes. Doubtless most of them began poor; now they are rich. This that they have, they earned. How excellent was the wisdom of the forefathers that established here the broad and unrestricted fields that invite and encourage gifted men! How superior to anything known abroad are these conditions of incentive and reward!

So I think, with a sense of profound gratitude

that I am of this country that secures these bless-ings.

But·am I right?

Hardly.   If I remain long enough in New York and gain instruction in things as they really are, there will inevitably befall me a sad and complete disillusion.   I shall learn that my patriotic en-thusiasm before the gleaming palaces was based upon the airy fabric of a dream.   I shall learn, perhaps to my dismay, that not one of the beautiful houses I have been admiring represents a fortune gained in any such way as I have fondly supposed, and not one of these fortunes reflects anything but discredit upon the national name.

The proprietor of the first house was not a great merchant: he established no mart, he brought to-gether no producer and consumer, he assisted in no way to supply any demand.   Wealth he has in huge superfluity, wealth that increases upon him until he knows not what to do with it; but not a dollar of it represents any service done nor any want supplied.

And the man that lives in the second house did not help to develop the railroad system, he has built no lines nor extended nor improved them, though he owns many railroads; he has in no wise facilitated transportation, but only made it difficult.

And the man that lives in the third house had nothing to do with developing the coal industry. Coal mines he owns, many of them, but he has never dreamed of extending them for the general good nor of making them useful to society. He has not made coal cheaper but dearer; he has not served society, he has injured it.

And the man that lives in the fourth house has built no great manufacturing enterprise, he has had nothing to do with any system whereby anything is supplied that men need. He owns great manufactories, but their product he has not made cheaper but dearer. He has not helped men to supply their needs, but only hindered them.

(Then how were these vast fortunes acquired? By what means were these white palaces secured? What does this wealth represent? How were the ability, energy, and foresight manifested? In just what way have the gifted proved their different molding from the ungifted?)

(One of the heroes of this field, a mighty general of these battles, one covered with the glory of innumerable victories, one whose gifts are deemed exceptional, whose ability, energy, and foresight

all men admit, has lately furnished far better an-
swers to these questions than any I can hit upon,
and furnished them under oath. He sat one day
on the witness stand, while a patient inquisitor drew
from him, reluctant word by word, the full story
of one of these great fortunes in the making, one
of these white palaces in the building. It appeared, to give but one chapter of his narrative,
that with three other men he had secured control of
a certain railroad: that thereupon they had arbitrarily increased the capitalization of that railroad
from $39,000,000 to $122,000,000; that at the
price of 65, which arbitrarily they had made, they
had sold the added securities to themselves; that
these securities thus acquired they had immediately
resold to the public at 90 to 96; and that from
these operations they had made a net profit of
$23,000,000.

It appeared further that in all these transactions
these gifted men had violated the laws and the con-
stitution of the State in which the railroad was situated; that their profits were utterly illegal; that
the additional capitalization was not needed for
any purpose of developing, extending, or improving
the railroad; that it had no significance to the prop-

erty except as an enormous burden that for years to come the public must bear.

But surely, say you '(still, very likely, under the spell of the old dream of *laissez faire,* still bewitched by the idea of the grandeur of fortune-building), surely, say you, this is very exceptional; men do not often make money in this way; the loud clamor of denunciation that followed this particular revelation showed how very rare such achievements must be.

Rare? says the initiated observer.   Not at all rare; and nothing is stranger than that there should have been any denunciation on this occasion.   It reminds one of what Macaulay said about the British public in one of its periodical spasms of virtue. Rare, are they?   Dear reader, some of the great, the very great fortunes of New York City have been the accumulation of generations through the gradual increase in the value of real estate; some have been inherited.   These may be omitted from the present consideration.   Aside from these all the stupendous fortunes quickly acquired have been gained in some such way as this captain of industry described on the witness stand; in some such way, because there is no other way in which they can be gained.   Nor, if convention be a basis of morals, does this way of gaining them involve reproach, for we have much more than condoned it: we have warmly lauded its results and agreed that the men that practise it are excellent men and model citizens; and doubtless it has been viewed abroad as the one distinguishing characteristic of our financial operations.

Therefore, without prejudice and merely as illustrations of these matters and as examples of the methods by which ability therein manifests itself, I purpose here to state some of the memorable achievements in high finance of that group of gifted men that formerly centered around William C. Whitney, and of whom the colossus and master mind now appears in Thomas Fortune Ryan.

CHAPTER II

THE BEGINNINGS OF A GREAT FORTUNE

HERE is a man whose career has been the romance of success, who has climbed to the heights of wealth and almost imperial power, a king of finance, a marvel of enterprise and commercial wisdom. He began poor, he is very rich; he began obscure, he is the partner of a king and the confidant of rulers; he was a servitor at a pittance, he is the employer of millions; he was an obscure and nameless molecule in the human tide, now he dictates legislation and controls policies, he commands enormous enterprises, he is known about the world, he is to the history of commerce as a famous strategist is to the history of war.

Surely this is a wonderful story. How admirably it shows the possibilities of that "free and unhampered opportunity" of which we have just spoken! The poor boy starting upon his career with no help but his own will and his two hands, with no advantage but the unrestricted conditions provided for him; and do but observe the fortune, estimated at hundreds of millions of dollars, the endless range of profitable investments, the huge industries that are now his! With no extravagance we may think that scarcely another man in the commercial world stands in a position so commanding. His mind determines upon a certain line of action, and the next day the poor cigar dealer in Australia or the cabinet of Belgium feels the effects thereof. In Kentucky and on the Congo, in London and San Francisco, from the northern limits of civilized Canada to and beyond Mexico, men are employed by him and are subject to his will; he says to them, Do this, and they do it. On the affairs of the nation he exercises a potent and constant influence. His own attorney is Secretary of State; he has his own men in the Senate and the House of Representatives; he has his own way about Panama Canal contracts. He can sway the actions, affect the voting, and lead the thinking of many thousands of men. He selects candidates for partisan nomination; men of his choosing sit in high places in local and other governments. Until very lately he was a director or trustee in thirty-two great corporations. He owns life insurance companies, banks, trust companies, railroads, mines, gas companies, electric light companies, traction companies; he is influential in the Tobacco Trust, he has won the control of the Seaboard Air Line. On the chessboard of finance he makes strange, secret, and astounding moves, and wins. Nothing important can now be done in that game without consulting him.

He lives most quietly in a great unpretentious house at No. 60 Fifth Avenue. In the mad rush to shower and splash the golden flood he has no interest. His life is business. He goes to his office early, he remains late; he works in his study at night. A tall, erect, powerfully built man, in the best of his strength; a very silent man, with no confidants nor close associates; a secretive man of whose plans and intentions nothing is surmised until they are recorded in events; a cool and self-mastered man that never says a word in heat nor does an act without consideration—Wall Street fears him and puzzles over him, but never understands him. He has a great square jaw and face as relentless as an axe, and yet his characteristic policy is to win by indirection. With hands and arms and skill to wield a broadsword his fancy is for the finest rapier. No man has more caution; no man

will thrust more boldly when the time comes, and for skill in extricating himself from a threatened position he has no equal in the Wall Street game.

He gives with liberal hand to church and school; his skill, tact, and measureless success are praised of all men. Newspapers pave his way with laudations. His word has boundless weight; with a sentence he stays a panic and helps to restore confidence.

Is not this success indeed?

Ah, yes; it is a marvelous story. Here was the poor boy facing the world alone, and none was poorer. The Ryans, an old family of Nelson County, Virginia, an old family of the indomitable Scotch-Irish strain, had been utterly ruined by the Civil War. The old estate swamped with debt; the wolf looking in at the window; the boy, sixteen or seventeen years old, left alone with his aged grandmother; the problem of daily bread real and uncompromising before them: all this sounds like the first chapters of an old-time romance, and yet it is but a recital of biographical facts. And there is more to come, as if culled deliberately from the roseate fiction of our youth. The poor boy, striving to battle with the depressing situation, wins his way to the great city (in this instance, Baltimore) to look for work. From one place after another he is coldly turned away. Still he persists. At last, almost at evening, he enters a dry-goods store. The proprietor needs an errand boy. He engages young Thomas, whose looks please him, to go to work the next morning at seven o'clock. Young Thomas takes off his cap and hangs it on a peg. He says:

"If you please, sir, I would rather go to work now," and seizing a broom begins to sweep out.

Does it not sound like a page from the old Fourth Reader?

"What are you doing there, little boy?" asked the good banker, looking over the counter.

"Picking up pins, sir," said Henry. And on the last page he is taken into partnership and marries the banker's daughter.

Do not smile. It is all sober earnest and part of the record of a sober, earnest life. The errand boy labors early and late at $3 a week. Presently he becomes a salesman. Then he is taken into partnership. Eventually he marries the proprietor's daughter. It is the very apotheosis of commercial romance.

Meantime, he had been looking far beyond Baltimore and the dry-goods business. From the beginning he had made up his mind to be, if possible, the richest man of his times.   Upon that determination the wide, square, bulldog jaws came down like a clamp.   It was the time of Jay Gould and Erie, of Jim Fisk and the first Vanderbilt.   The road to fortune was a turnpike to Wall Street.   His employer was interested in some banking and brokerage firm in New York; the young man secured a transfer of his activities from Baltimore to the golden city of his dreams.   There we find him in a humble place as clerk or capper or runner or croupier for some respectable house in the Street, and his energy, tireless industry, and profound interest in his work soon win him advancement.   No firm can afford to overlook the worth of a youth that does nothing but study and strive in his business.   After a time he feels able to make a start for himself.   He becomes a partner in a firm: Lee, Ryan & Warren.   Then he marries.   Soon afterward he buys a seat on the Stock Exchange.

Then came times bad for gambling—1874. Black Friday, the Jay Cooke smash and the collapse of so many fair firms were only a few months behind, and before was a long, dreary season of prostrate business, silent mills, and unemployed hosts.   Depreciated paper currency and inflated

credit had done their worst. Under such conditions, the public, having bitter memories and no
money to lose, will have none of Wall Street, and
the youthful capper finds but barren pickings. Yet
young Mr. Ryan, faring in a small, careful way
through those lean years, did well enough. He
saw his little operations slowly grow and the tilth
thereof was the accumulations that were the joy
of life to him. Certain qualities commended him
to men that sat in the high places about the Wall
Street game. He was intelligent, he understood
the market, he moved quickly—and he was silent,
always; a grave, self-contained, taciturn young man.
That was a great matter; anything once committed
to his keeping oxen and wain ropes could not drag
beyond those iron jaws. Gentlemen having delicate negotiations in finance found that Mr. Ryan
was a good man to operate through. He knew his
business and he could be trusted implicitly. He
began to win attention—and commissions; and
after a time he undertook some little things on his
own account that resulted well, both in profits and
reputation. He used to search out the properties
that were so bad that they must needs be remade or
perish, and to float with the upward wave when the
remaking began. He won no great sums, but was

steadily getting closer to the leaders that controlled millions and obtaining their approval as a young man of the right sort.

One of these leaders was of a mind and character unusual; the rest fade away into the dull mists of commonplace. In a time that has for its distinguishing trait the union of rotten business with rotten politics, William C. Whitney was a conspicuously able financial exploiter and a conspicuously able political manipulator. I suppose that without doubt he had the best mind that ever engaged in Wall Street affairs, and without doubt he was equipped for better things than he achieved. He had a big doming head, not very broad but long and high, strange blue-gray eyes, very cold, very steady, and utterly fearless; a masterful and confident disposition; and a knowledge of men, and I think contempt for them, beyond any other man I have known. He was at will the most fascinating and polished man of the world, or the most overbearing and intolerable bully. His associates always seemed to fear as much as they admired him; there are records of directors' meetings absolutely terrorized by his indomitable will. In his way he had extraordinary mental capacity; his mind was an unresting engine, his ambition was inordinate, and but for some providential tempering by spendthrift and luxurious habits would have made him monstrously rich. I need not pretend that he had any overnice scruples about methods. He could see a little farther than the grubbing moles about him, and discerning an object he moved relentlessly toward it, sometimes trampling heads and sometimes mire, and regarding neither.

Therein lay for him the talisman of ability, the badge that distinguished him from the 500,000, from the 1,500,000, and from the 2,000,000. The divine gift had this substance and none other. Mr. Whitney dwelt his days among the palaces; he was born to a sense of superiority; he married wealth; the burden of life was easy upon him. No one may say that the goad of poverty drove him to climb from among the 2,000,000 or the 1,500,000. But he was a conspicuous example of those that having means used wealth to get more wealth for which they had no need.

So many long-forgotten chapters of history hang about these records! The old New York Cable Railroad, for instance—how many years have passed since we have heard a mention of that once menacing specter, or of Charles P. Shaw, the eccentric genius that created it and with it scared New York from its rest? The thing actually had a charter covering almost every down-town street in the city and extending north to Yonkers, all to be operated by steam and cable. Only one other man in New York had looked so far ahead as Charles P. Shaw into the street railway possibilities, and that was Mr. Whitney. He had been Corporation Counsel of the city from 1875 to 1882, and among the things he had learned while in office was a respect for the urban transportation business. He made up his mind that he would get into that business and be rich. Shaw and his associates were exploiting the proposed cable road as a rival of the old Arcade scheme (of which a section was once constructed in lower Broadway), when Mr. Whitney forced his way into the concern He needed somebody to assist him in certain lines of endeavor, and for such labors chose Mr. Ryan. whom he made treasurer of the company.

Mr. Ryan was at that time nearing middle life and known among the discerning as one of the shrewdest and safest of the small operators in the Street. He had no foolish pride about accepting small orders, nor about performing duties not usually esteemed a part of the brokerage business, provided the orders or the duties involved proper recompense and the good-will of those that it was well to know. Furthermore, some advantages lay in his comparative obscurity and his silence. He practised assiduously the scriptural injunction concerning the intercommunication of right and left hands, and even at that time no one ever knew what he was doing until it was done. Hence he went upon any matter unremarked, and his noiseless and unobtrusive presence drew none of the newspaper or other attention that might be undesirable.

For years there had been talk of a street-car line in Broadway below Union Square, but the wise men of the city (of whom there was even in those days no lack) always proved conclusively that a street railroad in Broadway was utterly impossible because of the crowded traffic. Mr. Whitney and Mr. Jake Sharp were among those that scorned the arguments of the wise. Sharp was a heavy-jowled, heavy-bearded and scowling man of a type now practically extinct, part bullying contractor, part rough politician, and part shrewd and unscrupulous schemer and manipulator. It was a strange turn of fate that pitted this thick-skinned, crude and violent person against the polished and courtly Whitney. Sharp had long wanted the Broadway

franchise from Fifteenth Street to Bowling Green
for his Broadway Surface Railway Company, a
concern with a merely paper existence; Mr. Whitney desired it for the Cable Railroad   Mr. Sharp
won the prize—for $500,000 in bribes paid to the
New York Board of Aldermen.   The Cable Railroad is said to have made another offer, not quite
so good.   Mr. Sharp got his franchise and built
his road practically in a night.   He was a thick-
headed man of one idea, but he knew what an injunction was, and took no chances.

This was in 1884.   The next year Mr. Whitney
went to Washington as Secretary of the Navy in
the first Cleveland cabinet, but he retained his no-
tions about the street railroad as a source of wealth.
When, four years later, he returned to his active
career in New York, it was to lay hands upon that
very Broadway surface franchise that Sharp had
wrenched from his grasp—so strangely do things
come about in this world—and to get it for a small
fraction of the sum Sharp paid.   As he won this
long-coveted prize, he cemented likewise the most
remarkable combination that has ever been known
in our financial affairs.   Mr. Whitney had closely
observed the amazing achievements (to be related
later) of P. A. B. Widener and William L. Elkins

in the Philadelphia traction field, and he rightly estimated these gentlemen as desirable partners in his enterprise. With these he naturally associated Mr. Ryan.

The syndicate thus formed endured for many years, exercised almost boundless power, came, as we shall see later, to deal in many things besides street railroads, in more than one way became historic, and made more money, more easily, more rapidly, and on smaller investments than any other association of men ever formed in this world.)

Of these great deeds we shall have to tell hereafter. For the present I want to go back to the story of the Broadway franchise, because that contains matter highly edifying to all desirous of knowing the secrets of sudden wealth.

After Mr. Whitney went to Washington the whole scandal of the purchased aldermen burst upon New York. A public conscience that many persons had believed to be atrophied awoke to a violent if somewhat brief activity. Police Inspector Thomas Byrnes made a prosecution inevitable by wringing from one of the guilty aldermen (who happened also to have other black marks on his record) a full confession. The weapons of the law that it had been supposed could never be used

against bribe-takers were thus thrust suddenly into
the hands of the public prosecutor.   Many aldermen were indicted, many fled, three confessed, a
few were convicted.   Sharp himself narrowly
escaped Sing Sing.   Then, ostensibly as an act of
righteous retribution upon all this shameful misdoing, the legislature was cleverly induced to the
very unusual step of annulling the charter of
Sharp's company, which necessarily went into the
hands of a receiver.   The franchise was still there
and immensely valuable, but the company had no
legal existence and the railroad was operated by
another concern.   From this chaotic and ('as you
can readily understand) much depreciated state it
was rescued when Mr. Daniel S. Lamont, acting
for the Whitney-Widener-Elkins-Ryan syndicate,
bought the property for $50,000.

The history of public utilities in the United
States has always reeked with the corruption of
public officers, but it has few chapters that equal
the story of business politics in the Broadway franchise deal.   Previous to Sharp's victory the gift
of the franchise lay in the hands of the aldermen.
The way to get possession of the people's streets,
according to the accepted methods of the public utility corporation, was to bribe the aldermen to betray

their trust and (defrauding the people) to deliver
the highways to the profit-making of the corporation. Several companies (one of them a mere
blind for another) composed of gentlemen of the
most eminent respectability, engaged in a furious
competition for the prize thus to be gained by the
dirtiest and most injurious of all crimes. The bidding rose and rose until in the scramble bidders
and bidden alike lost their heads. Truly it was
a mad, mad race. On both sides all thought of
the statutes was forgotten while the companies bid
against one another and the aldermen raised their
prices. A more extraordinary spectacle has not
been seen in any legislative body; a mania seized
upon all persons concerned: there was scarcely any
concealment; you would have thought the selling
of votes was as legitimate as the selling of peanuts.

You that dwell where the public utility corporation does not rot out the soul of civic honesty, if
any such place there be, will find it difficult to think
I am not exaggerating; and yet I do but repeat the
records. The newspapers soon became well aware
of what was going forward. One Sunday afternoon a special meeting of the Board of Aldermen
convened in the New York City Hall. It came
not to discuss any measure of municipal legislation,

but to decide once for all which of the tendered
bribes was to be accepted; for how much illegal and
forbidden plunder the streets of the people of New
York were to be delivered over to an association
of eminent and respectable bribers.   Debate ran
high among men that favored selling their honor
to this company or to that; the relative advantages
of the different bribes were weighed and considered as if they represented legitimate transactions
in every-day business.   A reporter, going aimlessly
about, wandered into the City Hall and heard
voices raised in vehement discussion.   He turned
curiously in the direction whence the voices came.
They led him to the council chamber.   He opened
the door and stood there unobserved, a witness of
one of the most memorable scenes in American history—the open sale of the rights of the people of
New York to and for the benefit of some law-
breaking palace builders.

Soon the public as well as the newspapers became
morally sure that here was a huge villainy afoot,
but not even shame could stop the men possessed
of this madness for a share in the golden stream,
thus for a moment diverted from the palaces.   The
rival companies raised their bids.   At last one of
them offered to pay for the Board of Aldermen

$750,000, of which $250,000 was to be in cash and $500,000 in stock of the company. Sharp met this with an offer of $500,000 in cash on the nail. The aldermen, crazed with a wild savage lust for gold, snatched eagerly at the offer of cash in hand. Sharp won, the people's streets were delivered over to him, the bribes were pocketed. Very strange scenes were witnessed when the money was handed about among the men that had been purchased, and were thus revealed in the reversion to primitive appetites. Men went snarling and raging about the City Hall under the impression that they were to be defrauded of their share in the plunder then being apportioned. One alderman attempted with force to take another alderman's share, and in the very aldermanic chamber, practically in the public view, one that thought he had been overlooked assaulted the distributor of bribes and tried to strangle him.

But the franchise was awarded, the machine was set up for drawing from the pockets of the public the coins of which the palaces are built. When we come later to consider what the workings of this machine have meant for the 1,500,000 and the 2,000,000, it will be well for us to remember that its foundation was erected in the most appalling

public corruption known (up to that time) in this
country, and that the men really guilty of insti-
gating the corruption were never punished nor ever
in any danger of punishment, in spite of the explicit provisions of the laws that define and prohibit
such crimes.

Yet the painful fact remains clear to those familiar with actual conditions that all these incidents
represented only the culmination of a general system of debauchery that permeated most of the
legislative bodies of the country whenever they
had the power to give away the people's streets or
the people's highways. We that live absorbed in
our immediate affairs and guess the real life of the
country only when some potent phase of it is thrust
compellingly upon our attention, can have little idea
of the extent of these practices. But think for a
moment! Was it for reasons of morals or sanita-
tation that the railroad companies maintained lob-
bies at every State legislature in the United States?
Or do you think it really meant nothing that the
railroad interests interfered so persistently in party
politics and party management? I have seen the
head lobbyist of a certain railroad standing at the
door of a State political convention and with foun-
tain pen write upon a handy pad of annual passes

the names of all the delegates that would promise
to vote for the candidates. favored by the railroad
interests.   For twenty years there was in some
States of the Union hardly one political convention
in which the railroad interests were not actively
concerned and in which they did not win their way
by exactly these means.   Or, returning to the particular subject we have in hand, as a matter of fact,
how many gas, traction or electric light franchises
are granted on their plain merits as a surrender
of the people's highways to private greed?   How
many are secured without some application of the
methods employed by Sharp and his rivals?   And
finally, is there any spectacle more extraordinary,
incongruous and comical than we present when we
wildly cheer a public officer that undertakes to punish bribe-takers, while at the same time we stead-
fastly refuse to give up the obsolete and unnecessary
device of the public service corporation, the peren-
nial fountain-head of nine-tenths of the bribery and
political rottenness that makes the patriotic American hang his head?

CHAPTER III

THE FIRST DEVELOPMENTS OF THE FORMULA FOR SUDDEN WEALTH

IT is an agreeable dream to assume that successful men create their own occasions and with skill and mighty mind build their fortunes in spite of fate and circumstance; whereas there is no other lesson of observation so sure as this, that opportunity thunders long and loud at many a man's door before he wakes to have greatness thrust upon him.

Take for an example this public utility business that is the chief source of sudden wealth in America; for years and years it lay there in all men's sight and nothing came of it but the simple public utility. Street-cars were operated in this country for more than a generation before any one suspected that of all gold-mines the richest was concealed beneath the humble five-cent fare; and when the discovery was finally driven into the heads of men, the process was infinitely slow and fortuitous

36

and not due to any man's prescience. By chance and by circumstance the truth grew up, for the greatest profits of the public utility arise from its union with corrupt politics, and that union was an evolution and had nothing to do with any man's gifts. If the public utility had developed at a time when political bosses and devious financial games had been made impossible, there would never have been any great fortunes drawn from the street railroad business, ability or no ability, gifts or no gifts; a fact that might possibly moderate our transports as we contemplate certain of the glittering white palaces.

Philadelphia saw the beginning of the real traction industry of America, and the Centennial Exposition of 1876 disclosed the first sure glimpse of the golden treasure. Large numbers of people must be transported about the city; the horse-hauled street-car was the only vehicle for these migratory millions. Up to that time the street railroad had been by capital despised and by the public tolerated as a curious but necessary evil. The cars were slow and scarce; the service was in its infancy. In Philadelphia, as in other American cities, there was a separate company for every line of track, small companies of obscure and hardy investors; for to

capital sitting upon millions these two streaks of
rust and a jangling car that collected nickels seemed
too small to deserve the attention of adult financiers.   Slowly the fact became apparent that the
business was not really to be contemned, for it contained two elements that made it worth while.
First, it built up suburbs and had therefore within
it the power greatly and rapidly to extend itself
without effort, without care, without investment on
the part of its owners; for the more suburbs, the
more people were to be carried.   Second, it was
actually possible by debauching public servants, cor-
rupting politics, buying elections, and forming al-
liances with the bosses, to secure free and unrestricted possession of the public highways not for
one year nor for two, but for a hundred years or a
thousand.   A child might see that these priceless
privileges could be used toward fortune building,
and in a short time a child might also see that far
beyond even these bright prospects the true profits
of the business lay in the manipulating of securities
and not in the transporting of passengers, a fact
that will become more and more apparent as we
turn over these long-neglected records.

Into this fertile and lovely field came now the
men that long reaped its golden harvests. To speak

disparagingly of such success is a form of *lèse-majesté*. Fain would I say that the records of these achievements reveal remarkable qualities and amazing mental attributes, although it remains quite clear that up to the very gates of their good fortune these men were driven and thrust by fate. To the first of them, indeed, Charles T. Yerkes, belonged a certain combination of hardihood, audacity, dexterity, and persistence that was rather out of the common. But he had served some months as a convict in a Pennsylvania prison, and that experience had doubtless, and in more than one way, resulted to his advantage. It gave him time for reflection, taught him caution, and indicated how close with safety a man might steer to the reefs of the penal code.

In a measure Mr. Yerkes's trouble had been brought about by the Chicago fire. He had been in Philadelphia a daring young broker, and had won repute by successfully handling State bonds with the old banking house of Drexel & Company. With his prestige and magnetism he induced Joseph F. Marcer, who was then City Treasurer of Philadelphia, to invest money in Chicago. Some of the money, much of it in fact, was the city's. When the fire came it cleaned out Yerkes and Marcer and in that crash the theft of the city funds was discovered. Yerkes was indicted as accessory to the embezzlement, convicted, and sentenced to two years and four months' imprisonment; Marcer received a sentence about twice as long. Yerkes was pardoned after seven months, and returned to Philadelphia in nowise disheartened by his misadventure, for almost at once he resumed his labors in the financial field and began to retrieve his fortune.

You will find now in the best residence region of Philadelphia a magnificent marble palace, as grand, as imposing, as costly as any in New York or elsewhere, and surely one of the most beautiful of the homes of the fortunate. It contains a really wonderful art-gallery and many rare books and tapestries; it is one of the show-places of the city; the natives point it out with pride and strangers regard it with just admiration.

That house was born of the defalcation of Marcer and the plight of Charles T. Yerkes. It belongs to P. A. B. Widener. About forty years ago he was a young butcher in Spring Garden Market, in no way distinguished from two hundred other butchers there except that he took an interest in partisan politics, belonged to the political organization of his ward, and worked at the polls on election day. As a reward for these services his party found use for him as a lieutenant and lobbyist about the Pennsylvania State Legislature at Harrisburg, and when Marcer was removed from the City Treasury the young butcher got the vacant post. In those days the City Treasurer of Philadelphia was allowed certain fat perquisites. Hence it was a good thing, and when young Widener relinquished the office, he was legitimately the richer.

The butcher was a friend of Yerkes, who had also mixed much in the odorous pool of Philadelphia politics. Yerkes, being released from the penitentiary, looked about for something to do and stumbled upon the street railroad business. A piece of scrap-iron known as the Seventeenth and Nineteenth Street line was offered to him on credit at four cents on the dollar. He took it. The Exposition came on and traffic greatly increased. Mr. Yerkes needed money. It may be supposed that he badly needed money. Money was hard to come by. Mr. Yerkes tried a very doubtful experiment. On the rattle-trap contrivance he had bought he issued a small amount of bonds—about $200,000 worth, it is said. Very likely to his great amazement, he found that these bonds could be floated.

With the proceeds he secured another link of railroad and issued more bonds on that, and thus the whole system was started on its truly wonderful career through the choicest realms of finance. Mr. Yerkes had hit upon the great truth that in normal times somebody can be found to buy a bond on anything, and that with the power to issue bonds the gathering of great fortunes is simpler than the gathering of ripe apples, for they fall from the tree into your very hand and while you sleep.

When Mr. Yerkes had made the discovery that he could issue bonds on his scrap-iron, sell them, and with the proceeds buy more scrap-iron, he added to his original purchases, repeated the process, and in the end at a goodly profit sold the whole collection, scraps, bonds, and all. At that time, Mr. Widener, being no longer City Treasurer, was also looking for something to do. He learned from his old friend Yerkes how good the street railroad business looked, and with a few close allies, William L. Elkins, the late William H. Kemble, and others, he bought some scrap-iron on his own account. In a short time they discovered that all Mr. Yerkes had said about this business was true, and that still more was true, because upon them also loomed the dazzling prospects of the wealth that lies behind manipulation.

From this you are not to assume that these gentlemen nor any of them originated the Great American Idea in finance. That were to wrong history, to wrong the dead and them. They merely applied to their purchases the principles of that Idea after repeated exploits by others had brought it to the precision of a familiar scientific formula. It might be called the Agreeable Formula for Making Something from Nothing, or it might be called the Formula for Getting Rich by Levying Tribute on the Public. The essence of it is to gather money by compelling millions of people in this and succeeding generations to pay exorbitant prices for poor services. A simpler device never entered the human mind; of ingenuity or novelty it had just so much as there is in the pistol of a highwayman. To get control of one piece of street railroad, good or bad; to issue upon it all the bonds and stocks it would bear; to sell these, regardless of their real value, to the confiding public; to use the proceeds to buy another piece of railroad; to repeat the process as long as there was anything worth buying —what could be simpler? No risk was incurred,

no capital required.   The confiding public attended
to all that.

The Philadelphia gentlemen were not slow to
understand the good thing thus opened before them.
It was a golden snowball rolling down-hill and becoming an avalanche of money.   Each railroad
acquired by them in turn acquired another, without
trouble, without labor, without effort, and without
cost.   The owners of the device were made rich
while they slept; the entire population and all the
future labored for them while they toiled not nor
spun.   For every bond and every coupon on every
bond issued to buy these railroads the public must
needs furnish the money, now and for many years
to come.   But the gentlemen for whom the public
bought the road—they furnished nothing but their
agreeable presence and their happy homes.

For all this, of course, they had abundant warrant and shining examples in American financial
history.   Jay Gould had shown the precious potency
of the Agreeable Formula when he watered the
stock of Erie from $17,000,000 to $78,000,000
and made himself rich.   Since his achievement
practically every railroad corporation had followed
in his august footsteps, until to overcapitalize an
average railroad had become a far more important

source of wealth than to operate it. Mr. Yerkes and his friends imitated Mr. Gould and then bettered their instruction. Gould loaded two or three railroads with water and departed with the bagged proceeds. They made the loading of one railroad the means to secure a second and the loading of the second a means to secure a third, and so on until everything in sight was loaded—and theirs.

How easily this good thing could be worked was demonstrated by Yerkes's Seventeenth and Nineteenth Street lines. That grimy genius, Matthew Stanley Quay, who had an infallible scent for graft, business and other, succeeded Mr. Yerkes in the Seventeenth and Nineteenth Street lines, which he helped to "reorganize" into the Continental Street Railway Company. The Kemble-Widener-Elkins people "reorganized" their Seventh and Ninth Street lines into the Union Passenger Railway Company, with which, by the handy processes already referred to, they amalgamated one small line after another, until their system had swollen to a portly size. In 1880 they had accumulated enough watered stock to lease Mr. Quay's company. In 1883 they took in the Tenth and Eleventh and Twelfth and Sixteenth Street lines. Then they leased the Chestnut Street and Market Street roads,

among the most important in the city. The next
year they reorganized again, this time into the Philadelphia Traction Company; capital, $30,000,000;
nominal and ostensible cash investment, $7,000,-
000; actual cash investment, next to nothing;
profits, enormous; prospects, unlimited.

Good business. There were now in Philadelphia
three street railroad companies, and no more, the
many little lines having one by one been swallowed
by these anacondas. The Philadelphia Traction
Company next proceeded to swallow the other two,
and thus became possessed of the entire street-car
service of the city, 426 miles of rail. This, of
course, necessitated another "reorganization," and
equally, of course, another flood of water. "About
this time look out for high tides," says the financial
almanac whenever there is a "reorganization"
project about; "reorganizations" being invariably
floated into success upon huge issues of fictitious
securities. The syndicate's "reorganized" and
freshly watered concern took the name of the
Union Traction Company.

The history of this corporation for some years
eclipsed all records of fortune building in this country, and still stands unrivaled as a factor in business
politics. It has meant much more to Philadelphia

than a mere enterprise to transport passengers or a
mere enterprise to manipulate stocks and bonds.
Gradually the public utility corporations had come
to own the city government of Philadelphia just
as absolutely as they ever owned any acre of land
or team of mules. They elected city officers and
determined city policies. They maintained the
most perfect system for political corruption that
has ever been known among our cities. The rest
of the country has heard much about the "Philadelphia ring." The very life and substance of the
ring were the public utility interests and the fore-
most of these interests was the traction corporation.

Under the system the ring established there were
cast every year in Philadelphia from 60,000 to
80,000 fraudulent votes, and it was by means of
these votes that the public utility interests retained
their grasp upon the city government and upon the
privileges that made them rich. Every criminal
enterprise in the community had share in this colossal structure of fraud; the respectable stock company went into partnership with the brothel for
the maintenance of existing conditions. The money
that stole elections and stuffed ballot-boxes and
hired criminals to beat citizens, all to keep this

gang in power, was supplied by the public utility
corporations.   For years they systematically made
of the city government in Philadelphia something
before which all patriotic Americans bowed themselves in humiliation and unutterable shame; they
did it, these corporations by the public so foolishly
endowed with special privileges.

For years dishonest aldermen, crooked public
officers, election thieves, repeaters, floaters, thugs,
keepers of criminal resorts, the men that falsified
returns, were actively leagued with them.   Every
protected dive in Philadelphia, every illegal drink-
ing-place, every house of ill-fame, paid a regular
tribute to the ring, not in money, but in the votes
that kept the grip of the ring upon the city.   Each
of these lawless resorts was recorded in a list with
figures representing the number of illegal votes it
must furnish.   So long as it furnished these votes
it could continue to break the law; if it failed to
furnish these votes it must cease to do business.
From these illegal votes and others was developed
an autocracy practically as perfect as a satrap's.
No man could ordinarily be elected to anything except by the will of the men that wielded this power.

In all these operations the traction company was
most conspicuous.   It was to misgovernment in

Philadelphia what the Pennsylvania Railroad was to misgovernment at Harrisburg. If its sole business had been to make the American city a symbol around the world for all things detestable and dishonest it could hardly have done more to achieve that result. It has in its sinister history some of the most astounding legislation ever secured under any form of free government anywhere, and a generation of flawless administration could not efface the stains it has fixed upon the city from whose people it has drawn its countless millions of profits.

Such was the story of this development in Philadelphia, where, because of the vast territorial expansion of the community, street railroads were become an absolute necessity and where the Formula worked without a hitch. Some economies resulted from the consolidations effected and occasionally some slight improvements, but otherwise the public got nothing from the transaction except the pleasure of building the fortunes of the syndicate and the entrancing prospect of many bonds and coupons to be paid in the future. After a few years of these conditions only two defects therein marred the perfect joy of the syndicate gentlemen. One was that the motive power, which was still horse, cost sixty-five per cent. of the receipts, and the other was that no one could tell how long the people might submit to having their highways used for a private profit-making device. As to motive power, the overhead trolley was installed (against the indignant protests of the outraged citizens), and that not only effected a saving of forty per cent. in expenses, but built vast new suburbs to the increasing of business and the swelling of dividends. And as to the highways, it presently appeared that there was much to be said on both sides.

Here I must beg leave to digress for a moment into incidents.

To the foreign visitor, the long-suffering patience of the American community is an endless source of amazed comment, and perhaps justly so. Certainly, in no other part of the globe, so far as I have observed human affairs, would people endure what Americans daily endure of insult and injury. One might at times be tempted to think that they were obliged to submit to the extortions and mishandlings of their public utility corporations, that they had no means of redress or escape. How otherwise, for instance, could a foreigner explain the anomalous fact that the city in which the Declaration of Independence was signed had so long endured a tyranny so gross and bestial as the Philadelphia Ring?

But they might not always endure it, there was the point; they might not always leave the fortunate gentlemen in the quiet possession of these great privileges. So the gentlemen proceed to secure for their fortune-making a foundation that should be beyond all chance of disturbance. The public utilities combination had now far progressed in its arts of municipal corruption; it could, in fact, do as it pleased with the city government. It had elected the mayor and most of the aldermen; had chosen them for reasons of its own, and knew upon whom it could depend. A dummy company was formed. It applied for a franchise covering all the remaining streets, avenues, and alleys in the city. Mr. John Wanamaker, for patriotic motives, sought to prevent this outrage by making an offer to operate the public's traction utility for the public good. The combination's mayor, with ostentatious contempt, flung the offer upon the floor. The State Legislature at Harrisburg met one night in extra session. The enabling act necessary to the granting of the franchise was rushed through both houses, which sat up until three o'clock in the morning to pass it. A special train carried it to Philadelphia. There the city council was convened in a special meeting. As soon as the enabling act was received, the necessary ordinance was introduced, and passed, making to the dummy company a free gift in perpetuity of the public highways of Philadelphia. This done, the aldermen lolled back in their chairs and sang ribald songs. One of them long lingered in the memory of Philadelphia because of its chorus, which contained these significant lines:

Hail! hail! the gang's all here!
What the hell do we care? What the hell do we care?

Later, as might be expected, the dummy company sold to the Union Traction Company the amazing franchise thus secured, and the anxiety of the company was relieved; there was no longer any question about possessing the streets; it could go on to reap forever the golden harvest; it had won a great victory.

But now, you of the unable and ungifted, that make no profits and joy in no golden stream, how think you this momentous triumph was won?

The public utilities alliance had taken the money wrung from the people by one set of excessive privileges to obtain by corruption from the people's

epresentatives far greater and more profitable priv-
leges.   That was all.

A similar situation confronting the same interests some years later had slightly different results,
a fact that casts some doubt upon the perpetuity of
he Formula for fortune-building, and raises a
question whether the patience of the American people is, after all, eternal.   Among the vast concerns
of the gentlemen that operated the traction trust
was gas—the United Gas Improvement Company
being one of their business aliases.   About ten
years ago, under pretense of supplying a new and
better kind of gas, the United Gas Improvement
Company secured a lease for ten years of the city
gas-works.   By the terms of the lease a renewal
for another period was possible after the expiration
of eight years.   The question of renewal came up
in 1905 and the allied interests planned in their
usual way to add to their fortunes by securing a
lease monstrously to their benefit.

But the public discontent for once broke over the
barriers of custom and fraudulent elections, and
for once the allied interests were defeated; the force
of public indignation was plainly too great to be
withstood.   When mobs gathered in the placid
Philadelphia streets and with ropes in hand prom-

ised to hang the aldermen, there was evidently no
time for gangsters considerate of their own welfare
to be making further raids on the people's purses.
So the precious scheme lapsed.   In the height of
the trouble the residences of prominent men that
supported the gang were surrounded by threatening
mobs and for several days the inmates deemed it
advisable not to appear on the streets, a fact that
indicates the extent to which people were aroused.

This is the way the thing has gone in Philadelphia; it is the way it has gone elsewhere.   Rotten
business and rotten politics—the two are invariably
mingled in these triumphs.   Without the corrupt-
ing of politics, the sudden fortune builders could
never have obtained their huge privileges; without
their huge privileges, they could never have possessed their gleaming palaces.   So, flat-dweller
with $1,639 of total possessions, here is one way in
which the difference in brain-cells manifests itself.
Rather poor, it seems—does it not?—and cheap
and stained and tawdry look the gleaming palaces
so gained, when you think of stuffed ballot-boxes,
debauched public officers, and that soiled and
wretched alliance with the dive-keeper and the
brothel.   The man that lives in his little flat with
his $1,639 of total possessions and spends all his

days in this hard struggle with rent bills and
butchers' bills may never be nearer to a fortune
than the mass of his unable and ungifted fellows,
and yet he may feel that he has done nothing to
debase public virtue nor to lower his country in the
eyes of the world. And there must be something
in that; when you stop to think of it, there must
indeed be a great deal in possessing that conscious-
ness. We may doubt if there be anything in the
gleaming palaces that makes up for the lack of it.

But power! Those miles upon miles of great
sky-reaching structures massed solidly in the business region—we did well to take them for the em-
blems of huge, indomitable, irresistible, abnormal
power. And here are some of its manifestations,
strange and subtle. For what ordinary force could
compel a legislature to sit up all night and a city
council to meet in extra session that a monstrous
swindle might be perpetrated upon a community?

CHAPTER IV

THE FORMULA FOR WEALTH AS IT WAS WORKED IN CHICAGO AND NEW YORK

ALL this is to forereach a little upon my narrative. Long before the Widener-Elkins combination had secured a grip on Philadelphia, Mr. Yerkes, having enlarged in Dakota and Minnesota his experience with a gullible public, bent all his gained knowledge upon the street-car system of Chicago, which had never been exploited. He came to Chicago with $20,000, said to have been borrowed money, and asked for an option on some scrap-iron street railroad on the North Side. He found that some one else had an option that would expire on a certain day.

"At what time on that day?" asked Mr. Yerkes.

"At noon," said the cashier of the bank that was financing the deal.

Mr. Yerkes went away and on the specified morning returned with his $20,000 certified check in his hand. He sat facing the clock, which he watched patiently. The instant the hands reached twelve o'clock, he leaped at the cashier with his check. The option gave him the required wedge into the concern. In a short time he had hypothecated the stock, borrowed money on it, got more stock, secured control, started the printing-presses on a bright new line of stocks and bonds, and possessed himself of the whole institution; gaining moreover a surplus from which he repaid the $20,000 he had borrowed for the option, thus securing the property without investment or cost, which, I may say, is the universal rule in all these operations.

He now proceeded to apply his Philadelphia experience, issued more securities, bought more roads, milked them with construction company and other devices, and eventually, piling one corporation upon another and one "reorganization" upon another, emerged with the Union Traction Company of Chicago embracing all the lines of the city except those upon the South Side. As a concrete illustration of his methods and their results, I may say that the Union Traction Company was capitalized at $120,000,000 and in the height of its prosperity it was estimated by an expert examiner to be worth

as a going concern $16,000,000. Except for leg-
islation, aldermen, and newspapers, it cost Mr.
Yerkes nothing. As a system of transportation it
was the most picturesque lot of junk ever seen in
this world and furnished undoubtedly the worst
service.   Junk is the right word for it; Mr. Yerkes
said so himself. "The secret of success in my
business," he once observed, "is to buy old junk,
fix it up a little, and unload it upon other fellows."
I may remark in passing that there was very little
fixing up in the case of the Union Traction Company of Chicago. Why there should have been
any more, indeed, is not apparent, since the good
people of Chicago not only endured Mr. Yerkes
and his methods, but in fifteen years supplied him
with $40,000,000 of net profits on an investment
of nothing; with the which comfortable assets he
presently departed from the city that had, at such
an expense to itself, made him so enormously rich.
He used a part of the Chicagoans' money to buy
control of the underground railroad system of London, to which untried field he devoted his energies
the rest of his life.

But he had stayed long enough to make an enduring place for himself in Chicago's history. Only
one cloud there obscured his success.   The junk

that he manipulated was operated under franchises. That is to say that when the people of Chicago presented their streets to the street railroad companies, a date was set at which the right of possession should expire. For most of the roads the date was July 1, 1903, and its approach worried Mr. Yerkes. To his ability, energy, and foresight the expiration of the franchises seemed of very great importance. We know now that in this his ability, energy, and foresight deceived him, for it was of very small importance. The supposition was that when the date of the franchise should expire the people would resume possession of their highways and the companies would be unable to operate their profit-making devices therein. Mr. Yerkes and many others believed this to be true. It never occurred even to him that the colossal good-nature of the people extended to the length of allowing the companies to operate these devices without any franchise or other rights. Yet such is the fact. In New York we have seen gas companies continue to occupy the streets many years after their franchises have expired and have even seen the expired franchises counted as assets of great value. In Chicago we have seen a street railroad franchise expire and the company placidly continue to operate its cars exactly as if the franchise were still valid, defying meanwhile every attempt to eject it. Hence, Mr. Yerkes must certainly have been in error, and having once possessed himself of Chicago's streets, in all probability he could have continued until the day of his death to turn them into profits.

However, Mr. Yerkes thought it was necessary to have his franchises renewed and went sedulously to work for that end. The law of the State forbade the granting of any franchise for a longer term than twenty years. Mr. Yerkes went to the legislature, which he well knew how to manipulate, and secured the introduction of a bill repealing the twenty-year limit and granting him a franchise for fifty years. This was the celebrated Humphrey bill. A tremendous outburst of public indignation followed its appearance and its sponsors in the legislature lost heart. The bill was quietly allowed to die in committee. Mr. Yerkes waited a little and presently the equally notorious Allen bill made its appearance, authorizing the city council of Chicago to grant Yerkes a fifty-year franchise if it should see fit to do so. This bill was passed—in haste. As there was in the State of Illinois not one human being except Mr. Yerkes that desired to have it enacted and as probably there were very few that did not fully understand the nature of the reasons for its passing, the extent of the resulting scandal is easily understood.

The battle was now transferred to the city council. Mr. Yerkes had been long and skilfully at work and had secured a clear majority of the aldermen. He looked, therefore, toward an easy victory. But the popular wrath was aroused. The thing was too palpable, the corruption was too gross. Indignation meetings began to be held. The newspapers were flooded with protests. Spontaneously men gathered and declared that so monstrous a bribery was not to be endured. The atmosphere seemed stormy. On the night the vote was to be taken an immense crowd gathered about the city hall. It was observed that many men were armed and some bore ropes and clubs. The constituents of one alderman marched down-town with a band at their head, sent into the chamber, dragged out their representative and told him in the plainest of words what would happen to him if he supported the ordinance. There were cries of "Lynch them!" and "Shoot them!" Even sober-minded men advocated violence if the ordinance should go through. The gallery of the coun-

cil chamber was packed to its limits with an angry
and threatening crowd.   The evening newspapers
issued hourly extras; the entire city was aroused.
The aldermen looked at the sinister faces about
them and heard the shouts of the crowd in the
street and their courage failed them.   Men that
had bargained away their votes refused to stay
bought and the ordinance was defeated.

It had cost Mr. Yerkes, at Springfield and in
Chicago, close upon $1,000,000, and for his ex-
penditure he had nothing to show except some in-
disputable evidences of public hatred.   The lesson
must have sunk deep.   He never repeated the attempt to have his franchises extended, and when
he left Chicago the question of their future was
still unsolved.   Those that care to consider how
surely we progress in such matters may be interested
to know that the thing Mr. Yerkes desired and
failed to get has now, in the main, been secured
by Mr. Morgan and Mr. Ryan, and without any
riots, disturbances, or indications of public wrath.
All of which shows that there is more than one way
to pull off a rotten franchise.

One curious little incident never before published
remains to be told of these matters.   It may serve
to afford an instructive light upon the modern

methods of corporation campaigning. One of the
Chicago newspapers was particularly resolute in
opposing the Yerkes franchise ordinance. A trusty
agent of Mr. Yerkes sought the acquaintance of
the editor of this newspaper and endeavored to
induce him to publish a series of prepared articles
on the franchise situation. As these articles pur-
ported to contain furious denunciations of Mr.
Yerkes and his ordinance, there appeared to be
no reason why this newspaper should not use them.
But a little inspection showed that the articles asserted the existence in the ordinance of certain provisions that were not there. The intention was
to secure in a hostile newspaper the publication of
these false accusations so that Mr. Yerkes's newspapers could with a fine show of righteous wrath
deny and denounce them, and thus discredit and
discountenance the entire opposition. To discredit
whomsoever attacks them is the chief weapon in
the Vested Interest Armory. The editor examined the articles and discovered the masked ex-
plosive they contained. To lead the Yerkes agent
on, he pretended a hesitation about the matter.
Then the Yerkes agent intimated that the articles
would be well paid for. In the end he offered
$25,000. The offer was declined.

With Mr. Yerkes in the fatness of the goodly
Chicago harvest were associated his old Philadelphia friends, P. A. B. Widener and W. L. Elkins.
The only thing better than to own the traction system of one city is to own the traction systems of
many cities. So when Mr. Yerkes let the others
into the good thing of Chicago, all fared together
exceedingly well. Mr. Yerkes was faithful to his
friends and, in certain ways, generous with the
vast sums of money that rolled in upon him from
the pockets of the masses. He had a picturesque
way of dealing with aldermen, and then another
picturesque way of talking about his dealings that
rather endeared him to those that fancy cynic
humor. One of his compressed comments on a certain Chicago editor has passed into local history. So have other remarks of his. He cannot
be said to have originated the plan of running too
few cars and overcrowding these, but he certainly
gave that plan most extensive usage. Under this
system the cars in Chicago customarily carried
three times their normal capacity and the suffering inflicted as a result was great and general. The
people, whose patience is supposed to be eternal,
complained at last of this method of fortune-
building, and occasionally some one would arise

to remark that as the streets Mr. Yerkes was using for the purposes of his aggrandizement were really the people's, and as Mr. Yerkes was there by sufferance, it would be decent in him to provide tolerable accommodations to a public from which he was drawing so many millions. Some one actually suggested that Mr. Yerkes should run more cars.

"Tush!" said Mr. Yerkes when these matters were called to his attention. "It is the straphangers that pay the dividends."

Dividends, however, were a small part of his profits, the most of which were made in issuing and selling vast masses of fictitious securities and from construction companies that were supposed to do work for the traction company and really served as covers for the issue of more water. Two of these construction enterprises organized by Mr. Yerkes paid something like 500 per cent., which was cheerfully added to the load of obligations on the traction company. As Mr. Yerkes presently withdrew himself from the traction company, the extent of these obligations was a matter of no concern to him. I may add that the people of Chicago have found them of much more serious import, for upon them fell the burden of furnishing the dividends and interest on the securities thus created for Mr. Yerkes's profit.

I suppose that a device so simple and so common as the Construction Company Fraud can hardly require much describing, and yet familiar as it is to all that inquire into these matters it may still be something of a novelty to the generality of men. The essence of it was in this case (to pick one as an example of many), that Mr. Yerkes formed the Columbine Construction Company, composed of himself and a few friends. Then acting in his capacity as the controlling power in the Union Traction Company he made a contract with himself in his capacity as the Columbine Construction Company by which the Columbine Construction Company undertook, at a very high price, certain contracts for the Union Traction Company. The actual work could be and probably was sublet at a small price to some one else. If this arrangement seems in any way questionable I remind you that it is only part of a very general practice. At one time nearly all the great railroad companies, particularly those in the West, operated exactly the same device, and no especial criticism was ever directed against it. The officers or directors of the railroad company formed themselves into a construction company or contracting company, and then gave to themselves the fattest contracts that the railroad had to make. We are supposed of late years to have undergone some moral spasm in our corporation affairs, in virtue of which we no longer do the things we ought not to do, but within a few months, turning over the pages of the annual report of one of the greatest railroads in America, I discovered plain evidence that this particular Scheme for Getting It had by no means fallen into disuse. I do not know of any reason why it should. The money made by these methods is made from the stockholders at large in the first instance and eventually from the public. The stockholder probably never reads his annual report and of course the public does not know of the increased burden of rates that it pays how much is required for this or any other one item of gouge.

Mr. Yerkes, indeed, and all others that have pursued these methods might have plausibly fallen back for their excuse upon a practically universal custom. I would not seem pessimistic or given to flaw-picking, but the known catalogue of the "honest grafts" that railroad directors enjoyed in days gone by would make a total compared wherewith Mr. Yerkes's winnings would look small. Take

for instance, the various coal companies that the
Inter-State Commerce Commission proved to have
been the private graft of the officers or directors
of the Pennsylvania and reflect upon the methods
by which these coal companies were favored at the
railroad's expense.   Take the presents of Pullman
stock by which Mr. Pullman used to induce the
directors of railroads to make long time contracts
with him, favorable to his enterprise and costly to
the railroads.   Take the refrigerator car lines that
were (and are) the personal property of directors
and officers and gathered profits at the railroad's
expense—and the public's.   Take the practice of
placing new town-sites on lands previously purchased by strangely well-informed directors.   Take
the monstrous sources of profits in contracts for
coal and supplies.   All of these things had been
going on for years and were perfectly well known
to every person that dipped below the surface.
It seems to me in no way wonderful that Mr.
Yerkes should have managed to take his bit
with the rest.   It happened that in his case the
significance of these things to the public quickly
became apparent, while in the cases of the great
railroad companies the burden is distributed over
so many years and so many communities that

it long was unperceived. Yet of course there is
no more doubt in one case than in the other as to
whose shoulders bear the eventual load of these
clever maneuvers, nor from whose pockets comes
the money that builds these particular palaces.

I have been at pains to point out that the methods
of stock-watering employed by Mr. Yerkes in
Philadelphia and Chicago were not new, being, in fact, mere imitations of Jay Gould's
wizardry with the Erie. Yet it cannot be denied that the tremendous and conspicuous success (for Mr. Yerkes) of his operations greatly
stimulated the practise elsewhere and was to
a certain extent responsible for the floods of
water that presently inundated the whole field
of public utilities in the United States. The thing
was so easily done (in the lax way we have of car-
ing for our affairs) and its profits were so quick
and sure that it became the general practise. At
the present time if there is one considerable city in
the United States that has a street-car or gas service
operated on the basis of the actual investment
therein it is one of which I have no knowledge.
The introduction of electricity as a motive power
gave an infallible excuse for "reorganizing" the
existing lines, and so far as I have been able to

ascertain wherever there was a reorganization there was an issue of watered securities. It is a curious reflection that the patient people of the United States are paying in transportation charges and gas rates the annual interest on billions of dollars that never were invested in anything, and in fact never had any existence except in a balance-sheet, but there is no escape from that conclusion. The total steam railroad capitalization of this country contains probably seven billions, possibly eight billions of water, and proportionately the street railroads are still more heavily flooded. The total amount of the annual interest charges on these fictitious sums has never been calculated, but it is obviously enormous, and oddly enough it is a payment from which the public cannot possibly derive the slightest return, just as surely as it is the payment that enables these fortunes to be acquired swiftly and without effort.

Mr. Yerkes was undeniably a huge element for evil in Chicago, but some men liked him. They liked his candid, genial, and breezy conversation, and perhaps for that reason condoned in his career things not usually condoned nor discussed in a mixed company. But of Mr. Widener and Mr. Elkins no one ever knew much. They kept aloof

from the details and were known chiefly as recipients of the profits.   Both were very quiet men.
Mr. Elkins was retiring and eminently respectable.
He, too, built a marble palace that rivaled Mr.
Widener's; he, too, installed an art-gallery.   About
the personal traits of Charles T. Yerkes linger a
thousand reminiscences; about his companions none.
So far as any mark upon their generation is concerned they might exactly as well have been of the
unelect, of the unable and the ungifted that have
$1,639 of average wealth and fight the daily battle
in the little flat.

These were the men that now turned their attention to the street railroad situation in New York,
where, at the suggestion of Mr. Whitney, they
made their way through the basement door.

It was an inviting place to enter, and no one may
deny that fortune was grossly and blindly with
them.   New York had not yet awakened to traction
potentialities.   To the typical New Yorker a street-
car had always meant a funny little thing that ran
occasionally in a back street where there were no
stages.   He was just beginning to understand the
extent of that error.   And before he fully realized
what was going on about him, the fortunate gentlemen of the syndicate had made themselves very

much at home on the premises, where they fared
quite well, thank you.　By the application of the
Agreeable Formula, they succeeded in adding to
their frugal store one railroad after another that
had cost them nothing, until in a few years they
were in a commanding position in the metropolis
and exercising a very great and very subtle influence
upon politics and legislation.　I have yet to find any
instance where these delicate financial operations
have gone forward without affecting politics.　Tammany helped the syndicate and the syndicate helped
Tammany, and the fruits of this close alliance were
sometimes historic and nearly always a direct menace to the public welfare and the purity of government.

As to the historic part, I may recall here an instance that has too long gone unnoted.　In 1892
Grover Cleveland was a candidate for the Demo-
cratic nomination for President.　Tammany was
Cleveland's bitter, old-time and uncompromising
foe.　It fought him fiercely in the national convention, and when, despite its opposition, protests
and prophecies, he won the nomination, Tammany
went home swearing that it would not vote for him
at the polls.　But it did.　Like a quiet little lamb,
it marched up to the ballot box and cast its full

vote for Grover Cleveland, who received for President practically as many votes as Gilroy, the Tammany candidate, received for mayor.

This was, at the time, a political wonder of
wonders, and might well be, for it insured New
York State for Cleveland. The reason for it,
though obscured, was simple. Mr. Whitney was
managing the Cleveland campaign. Mr. Whitney
was also managing the Whitney-Elkins-Widener
syndicate in control of the traction properties of
New York City. He merely used the traction
properties as a means to induce the leaders of Tammany Hall to support Mr. Cleveland. That was
all. It was enough. Alike the Tammany bosses
and Mr. Whitney had too great interests in that
alliance to admit of any division over a little matter
like the Presidency.

As to the other phase of the matter, the syndicate
secured an interminable list of great privileges and
immunities to which it had no right, but by which
it profited immensely. Certain leaders of Tammany Hall became largely possessed of syndicate
stocks, and it is not yet forgotten that on a certain
occasion a large block of them was found among
the effects of a member of a certain leader's family.

From the beginning of its marvelous career in

New York, the syndicate was blessed with the sage
counsel and able suggestions of Mr. Elihu Root,
then confidential attorney to Mr. Whitney and Mr.
Ryan, now Secretary of State of this nation. Under
the guidance of this good man, the other members
of the syndicate could doubtless feel at all times,
and reasonably, that however unusual the course
pursued and however it might be criticised by a
harsh and unsympathetic world, it was at least not
pointed toward the door of the penitentiary. Anything that Mr. Root advised must be right.   Mr.
Root was accustomed to arise in Cooper Union and
other public places, and, with brow of thunder and
voice of righteous wrath, flay all forms of wicked-
ness, and particularly those practised by Tammany
Hall.   It must have been felt that ere such a man
would countenance the least compromise with evil
the heavens themselves would fall.   Hence with
bland confidence the syndicate gentlemen took Mr.
Root's advice, harvested their profits, and justly
esteemed their counselor.   Mr. Whitney said of
him that he was one of the most valuable men alive.
"Other lawyers tell me what I can't do," said Mr.
Whitney.   "What I like about Root is that he
tells me what I can do and how to do it."

Prosperity beamed upon the syndicate as one

property after another fell into its lap, without effort, without risk, without expenditure. At the end of its first ten years in New York City, the *World,* exhaustively reviewing the history of these achievements, declared that there had been added to the syndicate's traction possessions in the city $19,000,000 of water, all of which represented clear profits to the happy gentlemen, quite aside from dividends, interest, deals, and all other sources of income.

As to these other sources of income and some cognate incidents, these chronicles will have to say much hereafter, but for the present I may as well give two illustrations that, though small, may seem to indicate to persons in the 2,000,000 and to persons in the 1,500,000 just why they are classed among the ungifted.

1. Fulton Street is about a mile long, connects at one end with an East River ferry to Brooklyn, and at the other end abuts close upon a North River ferry to Jersey City. It is an important line of cross-town travel. In the late eighties the North & East River Railroad Company was organized to build and operate a street-car line in Fulton Street. One of the results of the Jake Sharp scandal had been a law, called the Cantor Act, by which

the public's franchises for public utilities were to be
sold to the highest bidder instead of being given
away by bribed aldermen. When the Fulton Street
franchise was offered under this law, competitive
bidding ran the price up to thirty-eight per cent. of
the gross receipts to be paid to the city.

The company was the first in New York to adopt
the underground electric system.   It failed, and
the franchise passed into the hands of a contracting
firm, Dady & O'Rourke, of Brooklyn, which completed the road and operated it, but with horses,
not electricity.   It was unprofitable chiefly because
of the heavy tax paid to the city.

At this juncture, about 1890, the Whitney syndicate came in.   It organized a new company called
the Fulton Street Railroad, and issued $500,000
of five per cent. bonds and $500,000 of stock, hav-
ing incidentally neither property, business, nor
rights of any kind upon which to base these securities. The syndicate then went to Dady & O'Rourke
and offered $150,000 of the new bonds in exchange
for the franchise and property of the old company.
This offer was accepted.   Mr. Whitney then used
his great influence with Tammany Hall and secured
the reduction of the tax from thirty-eight per cent.
to one-eighth of one per cent. of the gross receipts.

This done, the syndicate sold at par to the Metropolitan Street Railway Company '(which was the name under which it was then operating the street railroads of New York) the $500,000 of stock and had the Metropolitan Street Railway Company guarantee the $500,000 of bonds.

From this transaction the net profits '(without the investment of a dollar) were $850,000 made in a few weeks. The time was to come when it would look paltry compared with other gains of these fortunate gentlemen.

2. From bond issues made according to the Formula upon only one of the properties absorbed by the syndicate, the Houston, West Street & Pavonia Ferry Railroad, there was derived a net profit of $6,000,000. The ability, energy, and foresight involved in this transaction consisted in picking up the money. The service to society lay in loading an already heavily burdened enterprise with more obligations that the public must pay. Certainly, in these instances, the gifts of the gifted hardly shine forth as anything phenomenal; the brain-cells involved may be thought to be very much like certain other brain-cells of which we have a not too inspiring knowledge.

CHAPTER V

THE STORY OF THE GREAT MILWAUKEE DEAL

"IF Thomas F. Ryan," said Mr. Whitney reflectively one day in 1889, "lives out the ordinary span of life, he will be the richest man in the world."

Mr. Ryan was then a comparatively obscure operator, whose achievements in New York had been small and who, except for one thing, was chiefly remembered as the treasurer of Mr. Whitney's unsuccessful New York Cable Railroad.

But Mr. Whitney had other knowledge of Mr. Ryan. As soon as Jake Sharp had won the Broadway prize, Mr. Whitney dropped the cable project and wasted upon it no more of his good time, so that it lapsed into a thing for financial faddists and for the charges of the "black horse cavalry" at Albany. But when he saw his way back into the street railroad business and founded his syndicate and regained the Broadway franchise, he placed his greatest dependence upon Mr. Ryan, who became in all his deals his chief lieutenant and executive.

One reason why Mr. Whitney thought so well of Mr. Ryan was that Mr. Ryan had just pulled off a thing that showed he knew the Agreeable Formula and could work it as well as anybody else could.

On November 30, 1888, with Fahnstock & Co., of New York, Mr. Ryan bought the Milwaukee City Railway Company, the largest of the four street railroad concerns then in Milwaukee. It owned thirty-six miles of track, 700 horses, and 100 cars. The price nominated in the deed of conveyance was $1 and other good and valuable considerations; but the price on which the purchase was actually figured was $1,293,750. Mr. Ryan and Fahnstock & Co., applying the Formula by which Something is made from Nothing, property is acquired without cost, and fortunes and golden palaces are built in a night, immediately bonded their purchase for $1,000,000, and the next day, December 1, were filed the articles of incorporation of a new company with $1,500,000 capital, 4,000 shares of preferred stock, and 11,000 shares of common. This gave a total capitalization of $2,500,000, against a nominal purchase price of $1,293,750. In other

words, it enabled the purchasers to secure the railroad without expending one cent for it and also
provided a handsome balance in cash, or its equivalent, all furnished by the indulgent public—a result for which the Formula is unrivaled.   The
Central Trust of New York took the bonds.   There
were some claims against the old company, amounting to a few thousand dollars, that were assumed,
and some other claims that were not assumed.   For
these certain lawyers had bills to be settled, but
Mr. Ryan and his associates from New York came
into Milwaukee so quietly and did their business
so unostentatiously that they were gone before the
sheriff had a chance to serve his writs.

Eighteen months later, in June, 1890, through
negotiations conducted by Henry C. Payne, afterward Postmaster-General of the United States, Mr.
Ryan and Fahnstock & Co. sold the entire stock
of the Milwaukee City Railway Company to the
Villard Syndicate for about $1,750,000, a sum that,
in view of the bond and stock issues, represented
almost clear profits.   Later the Villard Syndicate
went into the hands of a receiver.   In the receivership proceedings the fact was disclosed that soon
after the sale of the Milwaukee City Railway had
been effected, the Villard Syndicate had offered a

very large sum to be released from its bargain and to be allowed to return the property—from which the actual condition of the goods delivered may be surmised.

Then where the gentlemen concerned in this typical instance got their share of It is clear enough. In the time that Mr. Ryan and his associates held the Milwaukee City Railway they did nothing to improve it. The community gained from their ownership no shred of advantage. They made transportation no whit better, cheaper, nor easier. They performed no service to society. They simply reached out their hands with the Formula for Fortune-making and drew them back with $1,500,000, which the people of Milwaukee must supply and continue to supply many times over. So you can see in exactly how much of utility or of public service lie the foundations of at least one of the palaces.

This was Mr. Ryan's first great victory in finance and it naturally gave him much deserved reputation. Mr. Whitney heard of the achievement and doubtless thought well of it, for it confirmed his previous high estimate of Mr. Ryan's capacity.

Nevertheless, for a few years Mr. Ryan's share in the actual steering of the syndicate was small, and the laying of the course was always in other hands.   But his time was to come, and no man alive was better able to wait, a fact that recalls another story, also with a moral.

CHAPTER VI

THE STORY OF THE HOCKING VALLEY LOOT

THIS is a little story of the Agreeable Formula as the veritable Philosopher's Stone of wealth, and how easily it turns to gold whatever it touches. It is especially commended to the attention of the flat-dwellers and others among the little able, because it contains many useful and informing lessons: one of them concerning the view that the courts have taken of some of these performances of the gifted, and another being the exact amount of ability required to make these gorgeous fortunes.

I suppose few of us whose memories go back so far will need to be told that twenty-five years ago the railroad system of the United States, which is now controlled by seven men, consisted of hundreds of separate properties, some of them exceedingly small and quite independent. Three of these little lines, the Columbus & Hocking Valley, the Columbus & Toledo, and the Ohio & West Virginia, ex-

isted in 1881 in the coal region of Ohio. Henry
B. Payne, Chauncey H. Andrews, Jeptha H.
Wade, and three other Ohio capitalists united with
one Stevenson Burke in a scheme to combine and
possess these properties—and others. Henry B.
Payne was one of the controlling powers in the
Standard Oil Company, from which he had drawn
an enormous fortune, and was the father-in-law of
William C. Whitney. He has also a kind of fame
in Ohio and elsewhere, through the charge brought
against him that he purchased his seat in the United
States Senate, and for other reasons not necessary
to discuss here. The other members of the pool
were rich, but not so rich as Mr. Payne.

Included in the property of the three little railroads were some coal lands, and coal lands are
always good to have. The gentlemen of the pool
earnestly desired to have the coal lands as well as
the railroads. Presently they found themselves in
possession of the coal lands, the railroads, and other
good and valuable things, and without expending
a cent therefor, or performing any labor, or making
any effort, or returning any equivalent, and yet
without risking the penitentiary. How did this
marvel come about?

In a very simple but effective way, as follows:

First, the seven eminent gentlemen forming the pool executed twenty-four separate notes, aggregating $6,000,000. These notes Mr. Burke took to New York, where they were discounted by the banking firm of Winslow, Lanier & Co., acting with Drexel, Morgan & Co. and the Central Trust Company. With the funds thus secured the pool bought the three little railroads and the coal lands appertaining thereto. The railroads they consolidated into the Columbus, Hocking Valley & Toledo, a name long and odorously familiar in railroad history, and the coal lands they reserved for other purposes.

Having thus secured control of the property, the gentlemen issued upon it $14,500,000 of five per cent. bonds, whereof it was announced that $6,500,000 were required to take up the outstanding obligations of the three little roads, and the remaining $8,000,000 were to be used for needed improvements, such as laying double track and increasing the equipment. At least this was the plain declaration of the resolutions of the directors authorizing the bonds and of the mortgage on which the bonds were based. There could hardly be framed in words a stronger covenant. Of the $14,500,000 bonds thus issued, $6,500,000 were duly used to

pay off the existing obligations of the three little
roads, but for a good and sufficient reason there
was no double-tracking, there were no other improvements.

The gentlemen in the pool had utilized the coal
lands that went with their purchase to organize another corporation—the Continental Coal Company.
They now exchanged the stock of the Continental
Coal Company for the $8,000,000 that still re-
mained of the newly issued Columbus, Hocking
Valley & Toledo bonds.   With $6,000,000 of the
bonds thus secured, they paid off the twenty-four
original notes that had been discounted by Winslow, Lanier & Co., Drexel, Morgan & Co., and the
Central Trust Company.   There was left $2,000,-
000 of the bonds, which they divided among themselves.

Their balance-sheet then showed an investment
of nothing, capital nothing, expenditure nothing;
net profits, a railroad system and $2,000,000—
which might be termed fairly remunerative work
and shows how liberally we reward the able.   Net
profits of $2,000,000 and a railroad are probably
more than any six or even seven flat-dwellers made
that year, but of course there is to be considered the

pool's services to society, presently to be disclosed in full.

The next chapter of the story introduces two additional characters. So evanescent is the glory of politics that I suppose not many men can now of a sudden find in their memories the face and fame of James J. Belden, of Syracuse; yet of old time he was a great figure in New York State and national politics and in that peculiar and unillumined borderland where politics and business fare hand in hand. "Jim" Belden, he was called; a smooth, suave, resourceful gentleman of a varied, sometimes picturesque, and usually successful career.

Mr. Ryan knew him well and he knew Mr. Ryan; they had reason to know each other, having some interests in common and very likely some sympathetic views. In 1889, it occurred to one of them, which one I do not know, that all the good things were not gone out of Columbus, Hocking Valley & Toledo. Wall Street knew pretty well the operations of the Burke Syndicate and generally believed them to be questionable. Not because they differed in their essence from one hundred other similar transactions by which great fortunes had been built, but because in this instance the thing had been done too boldly and with a brutal candor

repulsive to good taste.   Wall Street did not interfere with the achievement, because such is not its
way, but it held the game to have gone too far and
to be subject to investigation by the courts.   Mr.
Ryan and Mr. Belden must have become inoculated
with this view.   Mr. Belden went out into the
Street and bought $50,000 of the Columbus, Hock-
ing Valley & Toledo bonds.   Then he suddenly
brought suit against Stevenson Burke, Winslow,
Lanier & Co., Drexel, Morgan & Co., and the
Central Trust Company, to compel the return to
the railroad's treasury of the $8,000,000 in bonds
that had gone to pay off the syndicate's twenty-four
notes and had otherwise been used for the benefit
of the pool.

In advance of the bringing of this suit, Mr.
Ryan had gathered all his available means, and
very quietly, as was his wont, he had laid in the
stock of the railroad.   It looked like a good thing,
because there was no doubt that the original transaction was essentially dishonest, and if the courts
should so decide, the $8,000,000 would have to
be returned to the treasury of the Columbus, Hocking Valley & Toledo (where it was badly needed),
and the stock of that railroad would certainly go
soaring.   At the time the stock was inert and the

price very low, for the load of bonds placed on the
property by the Payne-Burke pool had almost
broken the road's back, and all it could squeeze,
gouge, and trick from the patient public (which
in every case pays for these amusements) could
hardly provide the fixed charges. So with cheer-
ful heart, no doubt, Mr. Ryan bought heavily. So
did Mr. Belden—quietly, always quietly.

Winslow, Lanier & Co. bitterly fought the suit.
On each side was a great array of counsel, and
without surprise we find our old friend Elihu Root,
now Secretary of State, fighting for Belden—and
Ryan. After profound argument, Judge Ingraham, who heard the suit, rendered a decision that,
while not regarded as determining definitely all the
points at issue, ruled essentially against Belden—
and Ryan. The ground on which Judge Ingraham
based his decision was chiefly this, that the money
the plaintiff sought to recover had never been
in the possession of the railroad company, but had
been appropriated by certain members of the pool
to their own uses. Hence it was not covered by
the mortgage and hence it was no concern of Belden's, whose claim was based upon the mortgage
and upon nothing else.

On appeal from this finding, the old General

Term practically sustained Judge Ingraham, though it severely denounced the actions of Burke and his associates. It excluded from any liability the banking firms from which Belden and Ryan expected to recover and restricted their action to Stevenson Burke, who probably had no such sum of money. It is proper to add that Henry B. Payne and two other members of the pool were exempted from the suit, it having been shown that they received no part of the plunder.

The case then went to the Court of Appeals.

But now a very strange thing happened and one for which there has never been any adequate explanation. To this day it remains among the historic mysteries of high finance. Just before the Court of Appeals handed down its decision in the case, there came secretly from Albany a definite rumor that the findings below would be reversed and that the majority opinion would be for Belden —and Ryan. I may say that it is not usual for advance information to leak out concerning a decision by the Court of Appeals; not usual and not proper. As a rule, the decisions of this, the most solemn and august court in the State, are an inviolable secret until they are officially promulgated. But in this case Mr. Ryan seems to have believed

that he had news of the impending decision, news
that he, most careful and deliberate of men, felt
that he could not doubt; and thus secure in his
ability, energy, and foresight, he bought more and
more of the stock, standing to make enormous
profits on the advance that was to be.

But when the decision came out, lo, it was against
him! That Burke and his companions had looted
the Columbus, Hocking Valley & Toledo of
$8,000,000 of bonds the decision clearly admitted;
but it held that since Belden had bought his bonds
with a full knowledge of all the facts, and subsequent thereto, and had bought them for the sole
purpose of bringing the suit, he was not entitled to
recover. Somebody else might be so entitled, but
not Belden.

Something about the decision always seemed baf-
fling and unsatisfactory. It was not signed by all
the judges and a story was circulated and eventually
printed that the judgment handed down was not the
judgment of the majority, that the advance report
that Mr. Ryan received of the decision was at the
time well-founded, and that the opinion rendered
was really the opinion of a dissenting minority of
the court.

All this helped Mr. Ryan nothing. His ability,

energy, and foresight had gone astray: there was
no rise of Columbus, Hocking Valley & Toledo
stock, no magnificent coup, no millions seized in a
day.   On the contrary, he saw the ship of his fortunes driving toward a lee shore, and it was only
by a changing wind that he could claw off.

As to the plundered Columbus, Hocking Valley
& Toledo, according to all precedent and all the
logic of the situation, that, being a poor staggering
concern overloaded with loot bonds and such things,
should have gone to the junk heap.   But in the
course of time there came a business revival through
the country resulting in an increased demand for
coal, and the wretched thing managed by sheer good
fortune to sustain itself.   Years afterward Mr.
Ryan hooked to it some more railroads similarly
broken-backed, blanketed these (if you will believe
me) with more of the handy mortgage, and in the
end sold the whole curio collection at a profit—a
consummation characteristic of the other side of
fortune-making, which consists of mere luck.

But as to the light in which the courts view these
performances, which was the moral we started with,
I cite these condensations from the scalding opinion
of the General Term, reviewing the methods of

Burke and his associates. The court found that these methods were chiefly as follows:

1. Purchasing stocks of other railroads and getting bankers to advance money on them by which the control of the roads was secured without further expenditure. In other words, the Formula.

2. Buying contiguous coal and other lands at less than their actual value and selling them to the company at a large advance.

3. Issuing the $14,500,000 of bonds for a specified purpose and then using $8,000,000 of the bonds for another purpose, namely, to redeem the notes given to Winslow, Lanier & Co., for the benefit of Burke and his associates.

4. Causing the company to mortgage all its property to support these bonds.

5. Concealing the use really intended to be made of these bonds and misrepresenting it in the covenant declarations of the mortgage.

All these actions the court held to be utterly wrong. How they could be wrong in this instance and right in the hundreds of other instances in which they have been used (to the decoration of upper Fifth Avenue), will puzzle the ungifted mind to discern. But anyway the gentlemen had got It and continued to possess It.

CHAPTER VII

THE STORY OF THE TWO VIRGINIANS

A THIRD instructive and moral tale might be used to illustrate the romance of modern business as well as the easy road to great wealth as pursued by the devotees of the Formula.

Here are two Virginians, two men of the good old Scotch-Irish strain, and they meet in a long, resolute, fiercely fought duel for a prize of property, one fighting with old-fashioned ideas of business integrity, the other with all the resources of the New Finance. What do you think? That ought to be worth while, ought it not? for it will show something about our new ways as compared with the old, and will reveal still further to the flat-dweller the paths that lead from his $1,639 perch to the high places of prosperity.

The financial agent of the Confederacy in the Civil War was a Richmond banking house of which an active member was Mr. John L. Williams, greatly esteemed through the South for his stainless reputation and his good works. He had six sons, whom he trained to his own stern code of integrity and personal honor, and of whom those that did not choose professional careers entered successively into partnership with their father. The eldest of these, John Skelton Williams, developed unusual capacity in revitalizing broken-down properties and in endowing them with both honesty and success. He did this for a piece of railroad flotsam that his firm had almost by accident become interested in. He put the thing together and made it go, and using it for a nucleus, began to add other bits of distressed railroad. He had energy and enthusiasm and profound faith in the future of the South. Thus he prospered with the South, and so did the banking firm of John L. Williams & Sons, Richmond.

This was in the early nineties. In the eastern part of the Southern country were then many independent short railroad lines, mostly indifferent and unprofitable. John Skelton Williams pulled together three or four of these, organizing therefrom the Georgia & Alabama Railroad with 460 miles of track, of which he was elected president. He added, in the next three or four years, other short lines, eighteen in all, built some hundreds of miles of connecting track, and made from it all the Seaboard Air Line Railroad, 2,600 miles long, of which in 1899, when he was thirty-three years old, he was made president, and thus became a powerful factor in the railroad world.

Mr. J. Pierpont Morgan was then paying especial heed to Southern railroads, and Mr. Williams greatly annoyed him by getting possession of lines that Mr. Morgan wanted for himself. At that time and for long afterward, Mr. Morgan and Mr. Ryan commonly worked together harmoniously, and Mr. Ryan found that by assisting Mr. Morgan's plans he was generally furthering his own. In this instance Mr. Ryan, acting for himself and for Mr. Morgan, undertook to get control of the Seaboard Air Line, and thereby block the Williams game. To that end he secured stock in one of the constituent roads and brought a suit (shown in the sequel to be baseless) the ultimate purpose of which was to prevent the consolidation and to oust Mr. Williams from his position. Mr. Williams went out with joy to the conflict; the legal battle that followed lasted for years, was fought with great bitterness and determination, and ended in the victory of Mr. Williams.

While this was going on, a curious incident oc-
curring in New York caused Mr. Williams (and
others) a certain degree of perplexity and might
have had serious results upon his affairs. The firm
of John L. Williams & Sons, Richmond, was closely
allied with the firm of J. W. Middendorf & Co.,
Baltimore, the two having joint interest in enormous development investments in the South, of
which the Seaboard Air Line was a part. These
enterprises were heavily supported and in part
financed by the Produce Exchange Trust Company of New York, of which John Skelton Williams was a stockholder and director. One Sunday
night in December, 1899, Mr. Williams received,
at his home in Richmond, a telegram from the secretary of the company requesting his presence at
a directors' meeting in New York the next morning
at nine o'clock. It was then after the time at
which the last train of the night should have left for
New York. Mr. Williams discovered that the
train was three hours late, caught it, and reached
New York at half-past nine the next morning. As
he was hurrying from the ferry to the meeting, the
newsboys were calling extras. He bought one and
discovered that the news was the collapse of the
Produce Exchange Trust Company.

This failure was and still remains a mystery of Wall Street. To all appearances the institution was beset by no storms that it might not easily have weathered. The Williams firm and allies would have been glad to secure practically unlimited help for it, if they had been informed of what was toward. Ostensibly and for public consumption, the cause of the trouble was mismanagement by the president of the company, one Beall, and its involution in the tangled affairs of Thomas F. McIntyre, one of the directors. McIntyre had plunged on the futile Flour Trust and lost. The Produce Exchange Trust Company had lent much money to the Flour Trust; but examination of the company's resources seemed to show that these loans were wholly insufficient to account for the failure. A few days later there appeared in the New York *Evening Post* a carefully written and, so far as one could tell, a well-considered letter from Norfolk, Virginia, in which the charge was made and maintained that the Produce Exchange Trust Company had been dragged down by the Morgan interests in order to embarrass the Williams-Middendorf syndicate, which controlled the Seaboard Air Line. I have not been able to find that this charge was ever refuted.

Mr. Edwin Gould, who had not before and has not since made the least figure in financial affairs, was the person that innocently pushed over the concern. He had just been chosen its vice-president, and was led to believe that the management (by Beall and McIntyre) had been very bad. When he had declined to go on unless these men resigned, and they had refused to resign, the collapse followed. An interesting discovery afterward made by Mr. Williams was that just before the suspension all the papers in the Trust Company's vaults that referred to the Seaboard Air Line, or to the Williams-Middendorf syndicate, had been removed to the office of some one in the Morgan interests. They were subsequently returned, but no explanation was ever afforded for this peculiar transaction.

For a few weeks the Trust Company was in suspension; then it resumed business. It still sails the financial seas, though under another name.

But to return to the two Virginians. Three years of fighting, fighting for business, fighting in the courts, and fighting off the flank attack made through the Trust Company, had ended in apparent victory for the Williams interests and apparent defeat for Mr. Ryan. But to bring the Seaboard Air Line to the full measure of its efficiency, ex-

tension and connections were needed, for of course
the Morgan lines continued upon it a relentless
warfare. The Louisville & Nashville was then a
big, independent railroad, owned by conservative
men who had no ambitions toward railroad expansion. It would make an excellent addition to the
Seaboard Air Line, and Mr. Williams and the
Middendorf firm quietly undertook to buy it. Before long they discovered that Mr. John W. Gates
was also accumulating the stock and had secured
enough, with the holdings of the Williams interest,
to assure control. At this juncture Mr. Morgan
discovered what was in the wind. The Williams
party had negotiated with the Gates interest and
had reached what seemed to be a definite agreement
by which the holdings were to be combined and the
Louisville & Nashville was to become a part of the
Seaboard Air Line system. Mr. Morgan, who was
then in London, was greatly annoyed and worried
by the situation. He sat up all of one night sending cable messages and receiving replies, that he
might prevent the delivery of the holdings necessary to complete the Williams-Gates deal.

At two o'clock the next morning Charles M.
Schwab, then president of the Steel Trust, in which
Mr. Morgan was the controlling factor, came to

the Waldorf-Astoria Hotel where Mr. Gates lived, awakened him, and told him that there had been that night a meeting of some of the most important banks in New York; that they regarded the situation as serious; that they knew Mr. Gates had purchased great quantities of Louisville & Nashville; that he was disturbing the market; and that they desired to know and thought they ought to know where he was depositing the stock as collateral. Mr. Gates gave Mr. Schwab the desired information, and Mr. Schwab went away. The next day the Morgan interests had certain conferences with the Gates interests, and the Gates interests notified the Williams party that they could not continue the negotiations concerning Louisville & Nashville. The next thing the Street knew, Louisville & Nashville had been sold to the Atlantic Coast Line, a Morgan road.

Thus the Seaboard Air Line was debarred from the connections it needed, and Mr. Williams was frustrated in the plans he had formed to develop the property to its fullest efficiency. It was so situated that if it could be supplied with outlets it could be made a great through trunk line of the first importance. Mr. Williams, undismayed by the reversal brought upon him by the secret maneuvers of

his powerful enemies, set about new ways of securing for his road the connections it needed. There
was a railroad that began nowhere and ended nowhere, but so lay that by building about fifty miles
of track at each end, it could be made a through
line from Atlanta to Birmingham, Alabama, and
thus furnish the Seaboard Air Line with a south-
western outlet. Mr. Williams bought this road
and began to build. At this time it is probably
better to omit the details of what happened next,
but there appears too much reason to think that a
plan, by no means unfamiliar in high finance, was
used, by which the work was made unnecessarily
expensive and Mr. Williams was deceived about it.
Anyway, the cost of the extensions far exceeded all
the estimates (just as had previously happened in
the case of the Third Avenue Railroad in New
York), and the Seaboard Air Line was soon in a
position where it must borrow money.

This was in the summer of 1903, when the
money market was abnormally tight. Financial
stringency temporarily settled upon the South. The
firm of John L. Williams & Sons had many lines
out. It perceived clearly that it faced a time of
trouble. Therefore, having made arrangements
to protect its interests and its creditors, it announced

in October, 1903, that it had suspended payments and asked for seven months in which to straighten its affairs. The creditors retained their faith in the firm, no runs ensued upon any of the firm's banks, and at the end of the seven months it fully resumed payments and business; but for the time being the financial prospects of Southern development looked dubious.

Things were in this situation when, one day, Mr. S. Davies Warfield, President of a Trust Company in Baltimore, of which Thomas F. Ryan had been a director, came to Mr. Williams in New York and said:

"I have seen Ryan."

"Seen Ryan, eh?" said Mr. Williams, who was not much interested.

"Yes, and I think Ryan is the man to help you out of your troubles. He sympathizes with you, and if it should be entirely agreeable to you to take the matter up with him, I think you can get from him whatever money the Seaboard may require."

Mr. Williams is not a sentimental person, but here was a fellow-Virginian offering the hand of Southern fraternity, here was a former antagonist coming (with a chivalry that seemed characteristic of the South) to the relief of a distressed compatriot: he admits that he was somewhat moved by a generosity so great and a fraternal feeling so warmly manifested. Gladly he consented to a meeting. It took place at Mr. Ryan's house. Mr. Ryan greeted Mr. Williams like a long-lost brother and spoke with strong feeling of the unfortunate position in which Mr. Williams found himself.

"You have done such great things," he said, "and shown so much energy and ability that it would be most deplorable if you were not able to go on with the Seaboard Air Line, and reap the just reward of your labors."

Then he suggested that they should talk over the matter with Blair & Co., which is a name under which Mr. Ryan does brokerage business. So Mr. Williams with Mr. Ryan saw Blair & Co., and Blair & Co. arranged for a loan to the Seaboard Air Line of $2,500,000, on ample security and the condition that certain changes be made in the Voting Trust and the Board of Directors by which the Seaboard Air Line was managed. There was a distinct and explicit understanding, Mr. Williams says, that he should not be disturbed in any way, that he should be free as before to carry out his policy, that the management of the road should remain as it was; but having advanced such a large sum, Mr. Ryan urged that it was only fair he should be represented.

Mr. Williams agreed to this and communicated with his friends, some of whom readily resigned from the board and from the Voting Trust, and other men were named in their places.

As soon as this had been effected, Mr. Williams observed a great change in the attitude of the new directors and quickly discovered that instead of supporting him they were bent upon thwarting him. At almost the end of December, 1903, they notified him that, with January 1 close at hand, there was no money wherewith to pay the coupons, that the earnings of the road were insufficient to meet the fixed charges, and that it would be necessary to effect a new loan of $5,000,000, of which $2,500,-000 was to be used to repay the loan of $2,500,-000 from Blair & Co., a transaction only a few weeks old. They had therefore decided to issue $5,000,000 worth of three-year 5 per cent. bonds, coupling them with a bonus of $12,500,000 of stock ($4,500,000 of it preferred). The bonds were to be offered to stockholders pro rata on their holdings. The so-called bonus stock, you understand, was a gift, or premium to induce subscriptions to the bonds.

To this proposal Mr. Williams objected vehemently, on the ground that it was wholly unnecessary. He was convinced that the actual situation warranted no such increase in the road's indebtedness and that if left alone the property would right itself. Subsequently, he discovered that the earnings showed a surplus of $400,000 instead of a deficiency.

When the directors saw that Mr. Williams was determined not to consent, they played their trump card.

"Very well," they said. "It is either this loan of $5,000,000 or a receivership. If you will not consent to the loan, we shall apply for a receiver."

Mr. Williams knew that in the condition in which his firm stood, a receivership and the consequent depression of Seaboard Air Line stock would be a grave disaster. He was therefore forced at the pistol's point to acquiesce in the loan, but he stipulated that the bonus stock should not be thrown upon the market, which was agreed to and understood on all sides. The loan was floated through Blair & Co., who were to receive five per cent. commission on all the bonds sold by whatever means, and who were a party to the agreement that the bonus stock should not be thrown upon the market.

Now, although the stock exchange lists were showing a strong recovery from the panic of the previous summer and prices were rising, Seaboard, through some mysterious pressure, was being forced steadily down, in the face of increased earnings.

Mr. Williams very soon discovered by indubitable means that the agreement about the bonus stock was not being kept. Bonus stock was coming out; he saw it with his eyes and handled it with his hands. He went to Mr. Ryan, whom he knew to be the principal in all these transactions, and complained. Mr. Ryan emphatically denied that any bonus stock had been sold. Mr. Williams said he knew better. Mr. Ryan said Mr. Williams was mistaken.

"See your Mr. Dennis," said Williams, "and question him about it."

"See him yourself," said Mr. Ryan, and left the room.

Subsequently Mr. Williams confronted Mr. Dennis, and Mr. Dennis failed to deny that the bonus stock had been turned loose.

He could not very well deny it, for the thing was palpable. The bonus stock continued to come out, accompanied by the most depressing statements from the new directors.

These statements and the flood of stock filled the air with forebodings of impending trouble. Under this pressure Seaboard Air Line stock was steadily hammered in the market until both common and preferred had fallen to one-half the price quoted when the new directors were chosen. Mr. Williams had long lines of the stock. In the embarrassed condition of his firm he found it impossible longer to withstand the pressure, and after a brave but useless fight he was forced to surrender.* His stock was sold for $3,500,000 less than it was quoted at the year before Mr. Ryan brought Blair & Co. into the property. Where-

---

*Mr. Williams may be thought to belong to the order of the Scotch-Irish that do not know when they are beaten. According to custom and the etiquette of Wall Street he should now have retired from the field and kept still. Instead he shocked and disgusted all conservative financial gentlemen by going on with his fight, even with broken weapons if he had none other. He used to attend the annual meetings of the Seaboard Air Line stockholders and render them memorable with frank, pointed and vitriolic remarks about the actual condition of the road. As he knew, one may say, every spike and rail in it, he was in a position to speak understandingly. Meantime he carried on his warfare elsewhere, and on January 2, 1908, he won a great and notable victory, as on that day at Richmond, Judge Pritchard in the United States Circuit Court appointed as receivers of the Seaboard Air Line Lancaster Williams (a brother of John Skelton Williams) and S. D. Warfield of Baltimore.

upon Mr. Ryan took possession of the Seaboard Air line.

One little incident I ought not to omit. In the midst of the stress and strain Mr. Ryan continued to express solicitude for Mr. Williams's welfare and a desire to help and advise him. Mr. Williams, fighting a big battle single-handed, was willing to be advised.

"Mr. Williams," said Mr. Ryan one day, "I have been thinking much about your affairs, and I see the way out for you."

Mr. Williams felt glad.

"The thing for you to do, I am convinced," said Mr. Ryan—and he paused impressively while Mr. Williams gathered new hope—"the thing for you is to go into bankruptcy."

But we started to find out where the gentlemen got It. These bonds, $5,000,000 of them, issued to save the Seaboard Air Line from imaginary disaster, bore interest at five per cent. With the bonus stock they were offered to the stockholders —the Blair-Ryan syndicate to take whatever the stockholders did not take and to receive, as a commission for underwriting, $250,000 in cash. Members of the syndicate are said to have tried to frighten and dissuade the stockholders from taking

the bonds. Anyway, the stockholders took only
$2,800,000 worth, leaving $2,200,000 for the
syndicate. Deducting its commission for under-
writing and the interest that the syndicate received, amounting to $450,000 in all, the cash that
the syndicate actually invested was $1,750,000.

On September 1, 1904, the Blair-Ryan syndicate's account in the transaction looked like this:

$2,200,000 five per cent. bonds worth 96	$2,112,000
35,200 shares of common stock (bonus) at 17	598,400
19,800 shares of preferred stock (bonus) at 33	653,400
Total	$3,363,800
It had paid out	1,750,000
Profit	$1,613,800

Or more than ninety per cent. profit on the
transaction. This is, of course, exclusive of the
profits made from hammering Seaboard stock by
means of the bonus issues.

From which the inference seems clear that one
of the ways to get It is to maneuver your man into
a hole and squeeze him, and another is to manipulate your generosity so as to get returns from it.

And besides the profits on these operations, Mr.
Ryan had the Seaboard Air Line.

Why should any man be poor?

CHAPTER VIII

THE OFFICE BOY IN HIGH FINANCE

"In this world," says the old philosophy, "man may not get something for nothing, but renders a return for all he may acquire."

But where? Not in the fertile regions of high finance, certainly. There to get valuable properties and to pay nothing for them is the essence of the game.

True, you cannot always play that game without disagreeable half-hours, but sitting tight and abiding in your faith in the American tolerance, you shall still win at the end. As you may observe in this story, told here to illustrate other phases of the ability that distinguishes the successful man in these pleasant regions.

In New York we have banks that are called banks, and banks that are called trust companies, the difference lying in a more liberal attitude of the

law toward the banks that are called trust companies. Many trust companies have been organized in the last twenty years, and some of them have
had historic careers. One, called the State Trust
Company, was founded in 1890 by Mr. Willis S.
Paine, as a kind of collateral enterprise of the
American Surety Company, of which Mr. Paine
was a director. The business of the American
Surety Company being chiefly to bond employees
and to indemnify employers, the premiums from
its policies constantly produced for it a considerable
stream of ready money. Now to have ready money
instead of credits to handle is a great thing in the
Wall Street game. One that has control of the
investing of much ready money can do well and
lawfully although the money be not his. The gentlemen back of the American Surety Company
thought it was a great deal better to invest the
premium money than to have it in a bank subject
to somebody else's investing. But the law rigidly
restricts the investing of insurance funds by insurance companies. Hence the utility of a trust company that is really a branch of the insurance company but operates under another name—an advantage thoroughly appreciated by the big life insurance companies in the palmy days before 1905.

The capital stock of the State Trust Company was $1,000,000, subscribed at 150, so it began business with a surplus of $500,000 in addition to its capital.

In order to secure permanently the control of the trust company by the insurance company, and to perfect the alias under which the insurance company was also to do business as a bank, more than one-quarter of the trust company's stock was held in the treasury of the surety company, and with more than another quarter there was created that beautiful and efficient device, a Voting Trust. That is, the subscribers to this part of the stock surrendered their voting rights to trustees that were bound to vote as the surety company might direct. Mr. Paine was president of the State Trust Company and a majority of the trustees were connected also with the American Surety Company.

For some years the State Trust Company sailed an even and uneventful course, being reputed a good conservative institution and performing agreeably its functions as the banking alias of an insurance company. In 1898 it had a surplus and undivided profits of $1,250,000, and deposits of $10,000,000, having paid six per cent. dividends and kept on the windward side of the law. But in that year the Whitney-Ryan syndicate, under the inspiration of Mr. R. A. C. Smith (a gifted gentleman with a career in connection with the business side of the Spanish-American war), secured possession of the American Surety Company and therewith, of course, control of the State Trust Company.

It is well to control a trust company that is making good dividends, but better to own it, particularly if you have many schemes and design to use the trust company as a financial adjunct of your scheming. The syndicate had the one-quarter block of stock. This it used as a nucleus. It then went to the other stockholders and persuaded or coerced them into parting with one-half of their holdings at 200, which was about the current price, promising that after the programmed reorganization the price would be raised to 400, so that the half each stockholder retained would then be worth as much as his entire holdings had been worth before. Next it effected on the Real Estate Exchange some ostensible sales of the stock (made by one syndicate member to another) at 400, which established a market rate at that figure. Then it borrowed money on the stock as collateral, at or near this artificial price, and with the money thus obtained it paid for the stock it had secured from the other stockholders—a small but pleasing illustration of the game before referred to, and tending to show that no man need go without any property if he will take the right way to get it.

Among the original stockholders of the State Trust Company and directors of the American Surety Company was one Abram Kling. He had 190 shares in the trust company and 400 in the surety company. He said that one day Mr. Ryan called him on the telephone and cordially invited him to sell one-half of his holdings in the trust company. He declined. Subsequently he gave the following version of the rest of the conversation:

Mr. Ryan—Well, in that case, Mr. Kling, if you refuse to sell, you understand, we shall have to remove you from the board of the surety company.

Mr. Kling—You go to the devil.

Whereupon, he said, he hung up the receiver.

Immediately afterward he was dropped from the directorate.

Mr. Kling clung (to speak in the manner of a conjugation) to his stock, and observed the sailing of the reorganized company. He may have had other motives than pure philanthropy; I do not know. It may be admitted that in these days pure philanthropy seldom journeys in New York below Fourteenth Street. And he may not have been the only person that for unpublished reasons regarded with suspicion the new owners. Anyway, neither Mr. Ryan nor Wall Street was yet through with Mr. Kling, whose name was destined in the next few years to become reasonably well known to both.

Meantime, the syndicate took possession of the ship and put in charge thereof officers dependable for syndicate purposes—Mr. Walter S. Johnston as president, and a serviceable secretary. On the new board of directors appeared the names of some gentlemen already well known to us—Elihu Root (now Secretary of State), Thomas F. Ryan, H. H. Vreeland (president of the Metropolitan Street Railway Company), William C. Whitney, P. A. B. Widener, and R. A. C. Smith. Of these, Mr. Root, Mr. Vreeland, Mr. Ryan and Mr. Smith were also directors in the American Surety Company.

The office of the State Trust Company was No. 100 Broadway. So was the office of the American Surety Company. So also was the office of Mr. Thomas F. Ryan. So also, pleasantly enough, were the offices of many stock companies, real, imaginary, plausible, potential, projected, prospective, and decoy, that the syndicate found useful to it in its business. The more companies, the easier becomes the application of the Formula for Wealth and the issuing of securities for other people to pay. Some of these companies were schemes of an exceedingly light and airy nature, having, in fact, no other substance than some sheets of paper. Captain Gulliver would have found much subject for remark among them, for they strongly recalled the Island of Laputa. They gave to No. 100 Broadway a certain distinction not, perhaps, wholly desirable for serious enterprises whose object is ordinary business and profits made in the slow old way that involves the rendering of something for something. The place was known as the "Promoters' Paradise."

Under its new management the State Trust Company seemed to fare excellently well. Its deposits increased; so did its loans. It gathered much money of other people for the disposition of the syndicate. It was known as the financial agent for many of the syndicate's multifarious enterprises. It was a bank of deposit for the syndicate's Metropolitan Street Railway Company. To the outside world it looked like a portly and well-conducted institution; inside its doors, as we know now, business went swimmingly and to the satisfaction of the gentlemen whose ability, energy and foresight had created much of the property out of nothing. In November, 1899, the State bank examiner looked upon the company's affairs and said that they were good, and the company's statement, January 1, 1900, showed that its deposits had increased nearly $5,000,000, for on that date it had $14,829,116.55 of other people's money to deal with and total resources of $17,122,411.57. Its profits in the preceding year had been $830,920.50, and it had paid six per cent. dividends. All was well, therefore, at No. 100 Broadway.

Suddenly, in the midst of this fair day and cloudless sky, a bolt fell. On January 11, 1900, Mr. Kling presented to the Governor of New York a long communication in which he made specific and very grave charges against the management of the State Trust Company, and petitioned for the appointment of a commissioner to investigate the company's affairs. He declared that the directors, in violation of the express mandates of the law, had repeatedly lent to themselves the company's assets; that they had lent money to themselves under other persons' names upon questionable or worthless security and upon none at all; that they had lent to individual borrowers sums in excess of the legal limits, and that their general course had been lawless and such as to imperil the safety of the institution and the stability of business. These charges, if true, were enough to send the whole board of directors to the penitentiary for long terms.

Mr. Kling not only delivered his petition to Governor Roosevelt, but what was still worse, the next day he made it public. The governor seemed to be much stirred by the revelations it contained. He declared at once that he must know the facts and all of them, and to that end he appointed as a special commissioner to investigate the company, former Adjutant-General Avery D. Andrews, of New York City. General Andrews had been Governor Roosevelt's colleague on the Police Board under the so-called reform administration of Mayor Strong, and in the incessant squabbles of that board had taken some part. In more recent times he became one of the directing spirits of the Asphalt Trust, rather unpleasantly prominent in the Venezuelan troubles. His instructions in the State Trust affair were to go to the bottom of it, "no matter whom it might affect."

Now the State Trust affair properly belonged to the official care of Mr. F. P. Kilburn, who was then superintendent of the State Banking Department. For some reason not officially disclosed, the governor totally ignored Mr. Kilburn and entrusted all his house-cleaning to General Andrews. Whereupon Mr. Kilburn started upon an investigation of his own. There were thus two inquiries proceeding at the same time, while the New York newspapers, taking the scent, conducted a third.

General Andrews finished first. His appointment was telegraphed to him on the 12th, and he began work on the 13th. His investigation lasted somewhat less than five hours. He then ceased from his labors and returned two documents. One was a report on what he had found, and the other was a personal letter asking to be relieved from further research in the matter.

This seemed to press and public a startling turn in the affair, and great curiosity was aroused as to its occasion. People generally felt that here was something exceedingly strange and even mysterious, and they desired to know more about it. The public curiosity was not gratified—at that time. General Andrews was relieved according to his request; no one was appointed in his place; his report was locked up in Albany; and Superintendent Kilburn's report coming in shortly afterward, that, too, was consigned to oblivion. In spite of all demands, the administration refused to make either public, or to give any idea of the contents of either, or to take any action on either. The only information disclosed was that both reports had found the company solvent.

Meantime, the third investigation, that of the newspapers, directed toward burrowing into the specific allegations of Mr. Kling, seemed to establish in the State Trust Company a condition rotten almost beyond precedent and lawless enough to demand stern retribution. Mr. Kling had affirmed many astounding things about the management, giving picturesque details and illustrations, and of these at least the following seemed to be undeniably true:

1. The company had made a loan of $2,000,000 to one Daniel H. Shea, and this loan appeared to be either unsecured or supported by very questionable collateral. On inquiry, Daniel H. Shea was found to be an office boy in the employment of Mr. Thomas F. Ryan and in receipt of a salary of $15 a week.

2. This loan was $900,000 in excess of the limit

fixed by the law, and was further illegal because it was really made (in violation of the express prohibition of the law) to directors of the company. That it was so made was explicitly acknowledged by three of the directors, who, upon the publication of these facts and upon some signs of rising popular wrath, returned to the company the shares they had received of the loan.

3. There was a loan of $435,470.48 on insufficient and doubtful collateral to Louis F. Payn, who was the State Superintendent of Insurance. The State Trust Company was owned by the Whitney-Ryan syndicate; so also was the American Surety Company, which, as an insurance concern, was directly under the official supervision of Mr. Payn and capable of receiving benefits at his hands, a fact that made this loan, which was improper in other ways, look and smell exceedingly ill.

4. There was a loan of $412,000 to William F. Sheehan, also on very doubtful security. Mr. Sheehan was, and still is, a person of great influence in the Democratic Party of the State of New York. He was also of counsel (though not often appearing in court) for the Metropolitan Street Railway Company and for Mr. Thomas F. Ryan.

There were reasons to believe that this was far from the extent of the questionable transactions.

Some of the journals now renewed their urgent demands that the State administration should make public the Andrews and Kilburn reports, or at least one of them. This the State administration still refused to do, although urged on every ground of duty and obligation, and although in the beginning there had been a promise that the public should know everything of interest concerning the company, and General Andrews had been ordered to go to the bottom of the inquiry, "no matter whom it might affect." Mr. Kilburn and General Andrews as steadily refused to give an inkling of the nature of their discoveries. A very strange but most potent spell of silence and inaction seemed to have mastered all the authorities. In New York City the district attorney and in Albany the attorney-general declined to act. A committee of the State Assembly was induced to demand a copy of the Kilburn report, but by the time it was produced the committee had voted 6 to 5 to return it with the seals unbroken. A demand for a legislative committee of investigation was similarly ineffectual. And against this blank wall official inquiry seemed to have come to an end.

Yet for some days the developments gave to the story daily a worse aspect. That loan to Louis F. Payn, for instance, seemed a thing that absolutely demanded more light upon it. Men recalled that the State Trust Company was owned by the owners of the Metropolitan Street Railway Company, and that certain advantages secured by the Metropolitan Street Railway Company at Albany the previous winter made it inappropriate for that company to deal much or openly with politicians. In those days the Third Avenue Railroad was still an independent concern and was engaged in fighting the Metropolitan. Both companies secured what they were pleased to call rights in Amsterdam Avenue and a furious battle began between them for the possession of that part of the people's highways. Mr. Payn was a political leader of much power in the State; that is, he was supposed to "swing" several votes in the legislature, where the deciding contest was fought. For reasons never divulged, the Third Avenue Company counted securely upon the support of Mr. Payn, and with the votes that he "swung" it expected to have a majority, narrow but sufficient. But when the final ballot was taken, the votes that Mr. Payn was said to "swing" appeared, to the amazement of the spectators, in the Metropolitan column, and the Third Avenue Company was defeated.

Soon afterward, a trust company owned by the Metropolitan Street Railway Company lent to Mr. Payn a very large sum of money on very inadequate security. To the average man this fact would seem to constitute a situation that no public officer sworn to enforce the law could ignore. Particularly when the money thus lent was not the money of the Metropolitan Street Railway Company, but of depositors that had innocently confided it to a trust company in ignorance of the fact that this trust company was an alias for a surety company, and the surety company was an alias for the traction company, and the traction company was an alias for something else. And again, particularly when such loans, made in utter defiance of the law, threatened the whole structure of business confidence.

In the criminal courts of New York City that month there were tried and sent to prison hundreds of men whose offenses against the law and society were trivial compared with these. Therefore, it appeared, the machinery of justice was in regular working order.

Yet in New York against these offenders would no man move.

CHAPTER IX

ADDITIONAL LIGHT ON THE JUDICIOUS MIXTURE
OF POLITICS AND BUSINESS THAT IS ESSENTIAL
TO THE BEST PLAYING OF THE GAME

BAD as all this was, worse remained behind. On
the 12th of March the New York *World* managed
to secure, in some surreptitious way, a copy of the
Kilburn report (so carefully suppressed at Albany),
and published it, practically in full. The whole
country gasped at the official confirmation it contained of the worst charges made by Kling or hinted
by the newspapers. There seemed no longer a
chance to doubt that the official investigation had
been muzzled because of "the prominence of the
persons involved," who now stood forth in a white
light, painfully conspicuous. They were:

Elihu Root, then Secretary of War, now Secretary of State, a director in the State Trust Company, long the personal and confidential adviser
of Mr. Whitney and Mr. Ryan.

John W. Griggs, then Attorney-General of the United States.

Thomas F. Ryan.

William C. Whitney.

P. A. B. Widener.

R. A. C. Smith.

Anthony N. Brady.

It appeared that of the $14,829,116.55 of other people's money confidingly deposited with this trust company, $5,133,270.48 had been swept into improper or utterly illegal loans for the benefit of the gentlemen whose ability, energy, and foresight had created something from nothing.

Among these loans were the following:

Daniel H. Shea..............................	$2,000,000.00
Moore & Schley.............................	1,000,000.00
Louis F. Payn..............................	435,470.48
Anthony N. Brady..........................	285,000.00
William F. Sheehan.........................	435,000.00
Metropolitan Traction Company.............	500,000.00

It appeared further that the loan to the office boy Shea had been negotiated by Elihu Root, director of the company, member of the executive committee, and its personal and confidential adviser, and that it had been kept off the directors' minute books.

"Beyond all question," said the report, "this loan was illegal, because excessive, and because, in part, it was made directly to directors of the company."

Illegal!   Well, is it possible to conceive of anything more illegal?   For how reads the law upon this subject?

"No loan shall be made by any such corporation [trust company] directly or indirectly to any director or officer thereof."—General Banking Act, section 156.   Passed in 1892.

And further:

"Every director of a moneyed corporation who wilfully does any act as such director which is expressly forbidden by law, or wilfully omits to perform any duty imposed upon him as such director by law, is guilty of a misdemeanor, if no other punishment is prescribed therefor by law."—Penal Code, section 603.

It appeared further from the report that the collaterals securing the Sheehan loan were "not currently quoted," and that Mr. Kilburn could not estimate their value, which was, of course, a polite way of saying that they were rubbish.   It appeared further that this loan was in reality made in the interest of—what, for a guess?   Why, our old friend the United Gas Improvement Company of

Philadelphia, the corporation that afterward became so popular that the people gathered to hang some of its advocates. The United Gas Improvement Company got that loan and was to repay it, presumably out of the money gathered in such questionable ways in Philadelphia. But the United Gas Improvement Company was the syndicate, and the syndicate (and Mr. Root) composed the directorate of the State Trust Company. So that when we have traveled the circle of ability, energy, and foresight we have nothing but the directors (in violation of the law) lending their depositors' money to themselves.

It appeared further that the loan of $285,000 to Anthony N. Brady was without security of any kind, and that Mr. Brady, who was and is the autocrat of that popular and favorite institution, the Brooklyn Rapid Transit, was the close associate of the syndicate in many of its operations.

And it appeared further that the loan of $500,000 to the Metropolitan Traction Company was without security of any kind, and that the Metropolitan Traction Company was the syndicate.

All this was only the beginning of the story. Examination of the collateral reported as securing some of the loans showed remarkable things. Thus, in the case of the loan of $435,470.48 to Louis F. Payn (who was perfectly well known to be of small means), the collateral had at the most a nominal value of only $350,000, so that $85,000 of the loan was not even nominally secured.   Most of the collateral that was deposited consisted of the so-called securities of corporations like the New York & North Shore Railroad, which, astonishing as it may seem, were the doubtful and obscure properties of the syndicate itself.

Hence, it was to be assumed that none of the securities deposited had ever been owned by Mr. Payn, and that the whole transaction was merely a blind to cover something else, some other operation, very likely with other people's money.   Nor is even this all.   Besides these alleged securities, which were to the loan exactly what a Raines Law sandwich is to a Sunday drink, there was a check for $100,000 made by the Metropolitan Street Railway Company to the order of Louis F. Payn, and marked "construction account."   But Mr. Payn, who is merely a professional politician, never had anything to do with any "construction" work for the Metropolitan and never could have had.   Moreover, it is perfectly well known that the "construction account" is among railroad companies a common and favorite disguise for rebates, graft, boodle and other illegal payments. No one could doubt, therefore, that here was something more than suspicious.

Nor is even this all. The check to Payn was an advance or an accommodation, and in the law of the State (the poor old forgotten and neglected law!) corporations are forbidden to make such advances or accommodations. So that here was law-breaking.

Again, the State Trust Company held $500,000 worth of the stock of the Metropolitan Traction Company, and, by the law of the State, trust companies are forbidden to hold, in excess of ten per cent. of their capital, the stock of other corporations. The capital stock of the State Trust Company was $1,000,000; ten per cent. out of that would have been $100,000. So that here was law-breaking.

And again, the loan to office-boy Shea was in excess of the legal limits. So that here was law-breaking.

And again, the last statement of the company declared that the loans on personal notes were only $10,000, whereas the loan to Anthony Brady and a loan of $70,000 to Miner C. Keith were on personal notes.   So that here was lawbreaking.

But, indeed, there seemed to be no end to the lawlessness that had rioted at No. 100 Broadway. Nobody believed that the so-called "Moore & Schley loan" had been made for Moore & Schley, and examination of the other "loan cards" revealed the names of many friends of the syndicate (some of them penniless) that under various devices appeared to have been favored with large amounts on syndicate or other airy collaterals.   All of these transactions had exactly the look of the Shea loan; that is to say, so far as one could judge, the obscure borrowers that apparently had been entrusted with great wealth were mere dummies or lay figures to cover further illegal advances to the directors of the company.   We need not here go into these matters, but I offer another list of loans and the securities therefor that will to the discerning tell its own story:

Borrower	Amount	Collateral
John W. Griggs	$14,000	Chicago Union Traction
John W. Griggs	8,000	Electric Storage

(Mr. Griggs was then Attorney-General of the United States. Union Traction is the final company by which Mr. Yerkes looted the street-railroad service of Chicago. Electric Storage was one of the syndicate's stocks.)

N. D. Daboll $35,000   1,000 American Tobacco

(Mr. Daboll was secretary of a syndicate company. American Tobacco is owned largely by the Ryan syndicate.)

Miner C. Keith $70,000   Unsecured notes

(This loan has never been explained. Mr. Keith was not generally known in Wall Street.)

Sharp & Bryan $100,000   Securities of various syndicate decoy companies

Henry P. Booth   60,000   Bonds of the American Mail Steamship Company

(The American Mail Steamship Company was a syndicate concern and Mr. Booth was one of its directors.)

Alden M. Young $76,000   Various securities

(Mr. Young was employed in one of the syndicate offices at No. 100 Broadway.)

W. A. Marburg $81,400   Chicago Union Traction

(Mr. Marburg was a director in the American Mail Steamship Company.)

H. G. Runkle $309,260   Chicago Union Traction and other stock

(Mr. Runkle was secretary of the American Mail Steamship Company.)

R. C. Peabody $80,000   N. Y. Gas and Electric and other securities

(R. C. Peabody was a brother of G. F. Peabody, who was a director of the State Trust Company.)

David B. Sickles $12,250   American Surety and other securities

Many of the securities supporting the loans made by the company were securities of companies floated by the syndicate or promoted by individual members thereof, and some of these startled the conservative element in Wall Street when it was found that money had actually been risked upon such stuff. Thus, one of the companies had no property, no rights, no business, and no existence except upon paper, and others were recognized as exceedingly dubious enterprises. A list of securities on which loans had been made by the State Trust was submitted to the loaning officers of four reputable trust companies of New York. Each declared instantly that his company would not under any circumstances advance a dollar upon such collateral.

One of the syndicate companies, Electric Vehicle, seems at the time to have had too little attention, for it played a momentous but silent part in the drama and had a history both interesting and illuminative.

Several years before the State Trust Company moved into the center of the stage, Mr. Isaac L. Rice, of New York City, became the owner of many valuable patents on storage batteries for electricity. To use them, he formed and was president of the Storage Battery Company, which had close business relations with the original Electric Vehicle Company. Between them a contract was made, stipulating that the Electric Vehicle Company should have the right to use the patents owned by Mr. Rice, and that the Storage Battery Company should furnish mechanical equipments to the Electric Vehicle Company at a discount from the market prices.

Among the ventures of the syndicate, which had now ramified in a hundred directions, it had secured possession of an electric automobile concern at Hartford, and it found, therefore, that it needed storage batteries. This drew its attention to Mr. Rice's company, and in a short time Mr. Rice found that the syndicate was undermining his control. He resisted, but vainly, and seeing what was at hand, retired to the Electric Vehicle Company, of which he became president, while the syndicate took possession of the Storage Battery concern.

Its first purpose, of course, was to get cheap storage batteries for its Hartford factory, but as soon as it was in possession it discovered the contract by which the Storage Battery Company, with its heirs and assigns, was bound to sell storage batteries at a cheaper price to the Electric Vehicle Company than to anybody else. This would, of course, defeat the very object the syndicate most desired, so the syndicate declared that it would not recognize nor be bound by the contract. Mr. Rice insisted (as was his indubitable right) that the contract was

perfectly legal and proper and must be enforced.
The syndicate gentlemen responded that they would
not observe it anyway.   A bitter row ensued.   Mr.
Rice purposed to enforce the contract in the courts,
which would probably have been not to the fancy
of the syndicate.   Anyway, Mr. James R. Keene
was called in to try to effect a settlement without
litigation.   He met the gentlemen of the syndicate, Mr. Elihu Root, their confidential adviser,
and Mr. Rice.   Mr. Keene considered the financial condition of Electric Vehicle and finally proposed a compromise that would secure Electric
Vehicle financial assistance and give the syndicate
in effect some of the advantages it demanded.   The
capital of Electric Vehicle was $10,000,000, of
which $4,000,000 in preferred stock was in the
company's treasury.   The syndicate agreed that
its Storage Battery Company should take over the
$4,000,000 of preferred Electric Vehicle stock then
in the Electric Vehicle treasury, at a price that was
less than its market value.   This stock was to be
held by the Storage Battery Company.   Then Electric Vehicle was to issue $2,000,000 of additional
common stock, which the syndicate was to purchase
at par, thus effecting to all practical intents an
amalgamation of the two companies.

Accordingly, on May 13, 1899, the Electric Vehicle Company issued $2,000,000 of additional common stock, which the syndicate took. It also possessed itself of the $4,000,000 of preferred stock that had been in the Electric Vehicle treasury. Instead of placing this $4,000,000 of preferred stock in the Storage Battery treasury, the syndicate placed there $2,000,000 of the preferred stock and the $2,000,000 of new common stock that had just been issued, and thus had the remaining $2,000,000 of preferred stock to manipulate. It was to carry out this deal that the $2,000,000 loan was made through office-boy Shea, the money thus secured from the State Trust Company's resources enabling the syndicate to make a $6,000,000 transaction and secure possession of the Electric Vehicle Company.

As an interesting corollary of this narrative, it may be mentioned that for his services in bringing about the treaty of peace, Mr. Keene was promised 2,500 shares of Electric Vehicle stock. This promise was never kept. Subsequently, without informing Mr. Keene, the syndicate made a beautiful move by which the $2,000,000 in cash that had been paid into the treasury of the Electric Vehicle for the $4,000,000 of preferred stock, was deposited in the State Trust Company, thus bringing the money directly back to the place from which it started. This working of the game, coupled with the refusal to pay him for his labors, undoubtedly nettled Mr. Keene. It was afterward asserted that he instigated the attack of Kling and secured the information that Kling laid before the governor.

There was still much more to the story of Daniel H. Shea, office boy. Mr. Kilburn in his report quoted the full text of the obligation on which an office boy secured $2,000,000. It read thus:

To the State Trust Company:

Gentlemen: Please take up and pay for 20,000 shares of the preferred stock of the Electric Vehicle Company which will be delivered to you by that company at par, and hold same for my account. I will reimburse you on demand for the amount paid, with four per cent. interest from the date of payment and all expenses, including revenue stamps.   Daniel H. Shea.

We hereby guarantee the performance of the above promise.

P. A. B. Widener,
Thomas F. Ryan.

On this extraordinary document Mr. Kilburn made the following significant comment:

"President Johnston testified before me that the guarantee was made at the time the loan was made, but by this I think he must have meant to be understood that the guarantee was made at the time the obligation was given by Mr. Shea and the transaction transferred from advances to loans."

Which was the only reference in the report to the highly interesting fact of the transfer from "advances" to "loans" and the only hint at another state of facts still more important. For the New York *World* charged (and was never contradicted therein) that the advance to Shea was really made at an earlier date, that it had then no endorsement of any kind, and that there had already been a default in the interest, which had been added to the principal.

Nothing but devious twistings and turnings whichever way one looked!

Mr. Kilburn, reviewing some of these things and obviously trying to put the best face upon them, says in his report:

"If the individuals merit severer treatment the courts are open, and public officials may be called upon to take cognizance of illegal acts."

But no public officials ever took cognizance of
these illegal acts, though repeatedly called upon to
do so.   Here were a dozen instances of open,
defiant, and wanton violation of the laws that
are made to preserve financial honesty and to
protect innocent depositors, laws fundamental
to the essential security of business; and yet
against the men guilty of these offenses not a
public officer lifted a finger nor said a word.
More than that, it was well understood from
the first that no one would be punished for these
crimes, and that so far as these offenses were concerned the law was a thing of shreds and patches.

And yet from the first there was a strange terror
upon all the eminent gentlemen concerned.   Mr.
Kling's petition was made public on January 12;
the newspapers began to get hold of the basic facts
in the case about the 14th.   On the 15th Mr. Whitney paid back the $300,000 that had been his share
of the Shea loan, and on the next day Mr. Widener
returned his portion.   It appeared that on the day
of the publishing of Kling's petition a frantic effort
had been made to reduce the Payn loan, and even
after General Andrews had begun his investigation
$100,000 had been hastily paid in to reduce the
illegal loan to the Metropolitan Company.   One

member of the syndicate, who had enjoyed much political experience and influence, sent a New York politician to Mr. Kilburn with an urgent plea that the superintendent should do as little in the matter as possible. Mr. Kilburn violently expelled the politician from his office. Yet the gentlemen could hardly have been in fear of the penitentiary they had earned; they must have known they were in little danger of that. Mr. Elihu Root, now Secretary of State, was daily in communication by telephone and otherwise with Albany, and the syndicate knew Mr. Root well and had a reasonable faith in his ability and success in such delicate affairs. It was something else that shook them all with visible alarms, drove them to restitution, and finally to the most extraordinary steps to cover their tracks.

Some of the men involved in the mess tried to bluff a way through the situation by averring loudly that the attack on the State Trust Company had been made to rig the stock market or was malicious and unjust. But reporters to whom these statements were made tell me the men that made them talked like men with unstrung nerves and that chill concern looked out of their eyes the while. In a way almost pitiable, they seemed to have lost

their heads, and in the stress of their painful situation to be no more "kings of finance" nor "captains
of industry," but very ordinary persons trying with
cheap and foolish devices to escape the consequences
of their own misdoing. In their confusion they
even attempted to defend the office-boy Shea loan.
First they said it was secured by a large block of
valuable stock, very valuable. What stock? Electric Vehicle stock. But as Electric Vehicle was
now known to be one of the side issues of the syndicate, that would hardly do. Then they said that
the loan was all right because it was guaranteed;
but a belated guarantee on a loan without consideration or real security, made by gentlemen that are
obtaining the proceeds of the loan, hardly seemed
worth bothering about. Finally, one of the officers
of the company said the loan was all right because
it was secured by a deposit of Consolidated Gas
bonds. This made a stir, Consolidated Gas being
a very valuable security. Investigation showed
that these so-called bonds consisted of promissory
notes issued by the Consolidated Gas Company,
when, at Mr. Ryan's direction, it took over the
New York Gas and Electric Light, Heat and
Power Company, both companies being syndicate
concerns, and that this transaction occurred subse-

quent to the Shea loan. What really happened between the two gas companies is too long and too remote a story to tell here, but the alleged interposition in the Shea affair was at most a mere matter of bookkeeping, was too late to avail anything anyway, and was, as a matter of fact, grotesquely absurd because the directors had made confession of the real nature of the loan when they made restitution—a singular indication of the fright that had seized upon the gentlemen making this blunder.

Further signs of trepidation were seen in the hurried rush of the syndicate to secure its fortifications at Albany. When Mr. Charles P. Bacon, Kling's attorney, found that Elihu Root had persuaded the State administration to take no steps in the matter, and that the prosecuting officers were resolved to protect the lawbreakers, he appealed to the attorney-general to begin an action to revoke the Trust Company's charter. To all impartial minds this seemed a reasonable proposal. The company had openly and in many dangerous ways violated the law. Nothing was clearer than that it existed to gather funds from the unsuspecting public and deliver such funds to the mills of the syndicate. As the law officers refused to punish the men that had done these things, therefore the game had best be stopped, the house closed, and the tools broken up.

But the syndicate's move upon Albany forestalled any such action—it has always had the most marvelous success in getting what it wanted at any seat of government, big or little. In this case the law department would take no action and the legislation demanded in the interest of the depositors was blocked by a band of expert lobbyists.

One of these, a man named Dinkelspiel, was particularly active at Albany in the syndicate's behalf. Mr. Bacon observed him at work one day and protested against his methods, which were exceedingly frank as well as energetic. Mr. Bacon said he would call the matter to the attention of the authorities and have Dinkelspiel put off the floor of the house. Dinkelspiel said:

"You make me tired."

Which, I suppose, was true, for he was never interfered with by the authorities.

The legislature declined to act in behalf of the public, and the syndicate put in its track-covering measure. It was a bit of clever bill-drawing, pretending to amend the banking act and really authorizing the State Trust Company to lose its identity by amalgamating with the Morton Trust Company, whereof the chief owner is Mr. Ryan. "The real purpose of this bill," said Mr. Bacon bitterly, "is to enable the State Trust Company to burn its books and destroy the evidence contained in them." But he wasted his breath in protests. Under the active guidance of the Republican whips, the bill went through with a rush. And so, behind the respectable figurehead of Levi P. Morton, the State Trust Company passed from sight.

And with it disappeared the evidence in the books. For this was what the syndicate, with such manifest signs of agitation, was striving so frantically to bring about. It had received one lesson; never has it needed to be taught anything twice.

As to what would have happened if Kling had not suddenly thrust his petition into the wheels, that is a matter of opinion. There is not the slightest doubt that the money of the depositors had been used to help the syndicate in some of the ramifications of its enormous operations. One may believe that the syndicate intended to replace the money it had taken, or one may believe that eventually, but for the appearance of Kling, the Trust Company would have been depleted and ruined. There are precedents for either supposition. But how-

ever that may be, this combination was caught with
its hand in the till and was obliged to make abject
confession, hurried restitution, and an extremely
awkward and humiliating exit from the premises.
When the man in your community that has prated
most about law, order, the welfare of society, and
the sublimity of honesty is discovered some night
in somebody else's chicken coop, he presents a very
unseemly spectacle, and so did certain gentlemen
of the syndicate.   When with much good-will they
kicked the obdurate Kling out of the American
Surety Company, they never dreamed what was in
store for them.   And when Kling, who had been
watching all the time from a crack in the coop,
suddenly leaped at them out of the dark with a
constable, there was a shriek of agony and such
genuine terror that it was literally a trembling syndicate the constable held up to the world's scornful
gaze.

But what was it that the gentlemen were so much
afraid of?

Let us not consider too curiously of this, but fix
our admiring attention on the services to society
and the ability, energy, and foresight involved in
breaking the law, evading prosecution, and divert-

ing to our own profit the money entrusted to us by others.   For therein lies much instruction concerning the golden palace and other subjects pertinent to this inquiry.

CHAPTER X

TOBACCO AND HIGH FINANCE

ABILITY, energy, foresight! Upon this blessed trinity we believe to rest the beautiful palaces, the spacious pleasures, the vast and swelling fortunes of the 10,000; from this origin comes the golden tide on which so gloriously they sail. Ability, energy, foresight! Precious qualities, for the lack whereof the 1,500,000 flat-dwellers and the 2,000,-000 below them must be condemned forever and irretrievably to their respective stations.

So we are accustomed to think. Perhaps we shall understand more clearly the difference between flat-dweller and palace-builder if we consider impartially the history of a very successful and in some ways a typical instance of the centralizing of capital, the American Tobacco Trust.

This institution dates back to 1890, and really owes its existence to the growth of the cigarette habit that infected this country after the Centennial

Exposition of 1876, when the cigarette was obligingly exhibited to us by some of our admired foreign visitors. By 1885 many houses were engaged in supplying the rapidly growing demand. These houses competed—and, in the end, extravagantly, so that none of them could make money. Five of the leading cigarette-making firms, to wit: W. Duke, Sons & Co., of Durham, N. C.; Allen & Ginter, of Richmond; Goodwin & Co., and the Kinney Tobacco Company, of New York; W. S. Kimball & Co., of Rochester, N. Y., and Oxford, N. C., met in New York in January, 1890, to consider ways of limiting competition. With no intention to speak unfairly or disparagingly, I suppose it was as commonplace a lot of men as ever got together. Some of them had been moderately prosperous, some had been in business a very long time and had little to show for it, and at least one of them was hard upon the shoals and had out the kites of many notes.

But they met and stumbled upon a plan of organization, modeled baldly upon a hundred other such combinations then and now in existence. This American Tobacco Company was launched (congenially) in New Jersey, where it put to sea January 31, 1890. Capital, $25,000,000; assets,

chiefly speculative and paper; investment, nothing
—literally nothing, for the men that formed the
company did not contribute one cent of money to it.
They put in their respective and unprofitable businesses, but these, while important to the total cigarette product of the country, were trifling compared
with the total tobacco manufacture.   Of the capital stock, $2,000,000 was set aside for what were
called the "live assets" of the five combining firms.
Nobody ever knew what "live assets" meant; for
the total real estate, free and otherwise, of all the
firms (if you will believe me) amounted to no more
than $400,000, and the value of all the real estate,
machinery, tobacco and cash was, according to one
statement, about $1,000,000.

Of the remaining stock a little less than $23,-
000,000 was distributed among the firms.   If a
sworn statement subsequently made be true we may
derive from these proceedings a pleasing illustration
of ability, energy and foresight, because according
to this statement the apportionment was effected
by the gentlemen present writing figures on slips
of paper that were deposited in a hat, shaken and
drawn out.   According to another, and an *ex-parte*
statement, the apportionment was reached after
"hard bargaining."   However this may be, the

watermelon was cut, Allen & Ginter and the Duke firm receiving $7,499,000 each and the other firms $2,499,000 each.

The firms then put part of their holdings on the market—which they could easily do without impairing their control of the enterprise. They found that the public could be induced to buy the stock at 117. In a day, therefore, without effort, without investment, without expenditure or risk, they had been presented with millions and had still their business exactly as before, only better, because now competition among them was eliminated.

From the first the new Trust was blessed with a singular and certain instrument of prosperity that lay in a fixed habit of the American cigarette smoker. No cigarette consumer ever went into a shop and asked merely for a package of cigarettes, but invariably he demanded a certain brand. As a rule he would not be content with anything but this brand; hence every dealer was compelled to maintain stocks of all the brands most called for.

This one little fact made treasures for the American Tobacco Trust and would have made them if the managers of the Trust had been wholly incompetent. The Trust controlled the supplies of many of the most popular brands, "Sweet Caporal," "Old

Judge," "Richmond Straight Cut," and the like.
Dealers must have these or cease from business.
Here was a power incalculable. The Trust was
engaged in suppressing its competitors. Any dealer
that would not help its cause it could practically
ruin by refusing to sell him the goods he must have.

Another powerful factor making for its prosperity lay in its opportunities to affect its securities
in the stock market, of which it may be well to cite
here one illustration from the records. In December, 1895, after a meeting of the directors of the
American Tobacco Company, it was announced to
the public that, owing to the unsatisfactory condition of the business, the usual semi-annual dividend
must needs be passed. Instantly, down crashed the
stock, the price declining in a few days from 117 to
63, assisted in its downward course by the gloomy
statements of the men on the inside of the company's affairs.

When the stock would decline no more, the men
on the inside loaded up with all of the stock they
could get—at bottom prices.

Soon after, the directors met and declared a cash
dividend of twenty per cent. and a scrip (watered
stock) dividend of another twenty per cent.

At this astounding news, the stock rose with a

bound. Up and up it went among the stars, flying higher day by day. When it hovered at 180 or thereabouts, the men on the inside unloaded the stock they had bought at 63 and reaped large profits.

The scrip they had issued as a dividend bore six per cent. interest guaranteed. Its only purpose was that the men in charge of the property should make to themselves a present of millions out of the enforced contributions of tobacco consumers and retailers.

Repeated financiering of this kind gave to the stock a bad name among conservative brokers and bankers, who looked upon it with uneasiness and rejected it as collateral except upon great margins. But the operation drew additional strength for the American Tobacco Company as one competitor after another was allured by these fabulous profits.

There were still left many strong competitors that would not surrender to either force or allurement, and most prominent among them was the great Liggett & Myers firm of St. Louis. Against these opponents the Trust waged a long, bitter and costly war. The scope of its operations had been greatly enlarged by the firms that had joined it; smoking and chewing tobacco had been added, and later it absorbed the snuff and cigar industries; but the hot center of its fight with Liggett & Myers continued to be over plug tobacco.

Liggett & Myers had a brand of plug called "Star," which was very popular. To oppose this the Trust put forth a brand called "Battle Axe," and to push "Battle Axe" into favor and oust the "Star" the Trust lost $1,000,000 a year.

The president of the American Tobacco Company and the originator of the brilliant "Battle Axe" idea was J. B. Duke. The treasurer was George Arents, of the brokerage firm of Arents & Young, Wall Street. Early in 1898 James R. Keene gathered certain facts in regard to the company's business and politics, and concluded that the losses had been great and unnecessary, and that if the $1,000,000 a year "Battle Axe" drain were eliminated and the enterprise put upon a straight business basis the company could water its stock to the extent of doubling its capitalization and could still make ten per cent. dividends.

As to Liggett & Myers, Keene learned that the warfare was wholly needless, because Liggett & Myers would consent to a union of plug manufacturers providing the officers of the American Tobacco Company had nothing to do with it. Keene determined to secure a majority of the $17,900,000 of the common stock of the American Tobacco Company, with enough of the preferred to give control of the property, then to depose Duke and Arents, organize a new concern to be called the Continental Tobacco Company, so as to take in Liggett & Myers, P. J. Sorg, the Drummond Tobacco Company, and other producers of plug, and thus gain peacefully and inexpensively the ends that the blundering Trust was trying to secure with war and money.

Mr. Keene brought in to help him Oliver H. Payne, of the Standard Oil crowd, who was William C. Whitney's brother-in-law; Herbert C. Terrell, afterward confidential attorney for the president of the Sugar Trust; and Moore & Schley. It was just before the Spanish-American War, and the whole market was depressed. Mr. Keene and his associates went quietly at their work, and so adroitly gathered in the stock that the men on the inside of the company's affairs never suspected what was happening. When the books closed and the happy gentlemen suddenly awoke to find themselves defeated and menaced with the imminent loss of their ship, the price of common stock roamed as high as

$800 for 100 shares overnight—that is, for the leasing of stock for election purposes.

The Keene associates got the bulk of their stock at about 90. Their purpose was to put it up to 200 and then issue the water. It rose rapidly to well above par, and all looked favorable for plan and planners. Keene's first determination, upon which he was wholly fixed, was to remove Duke and Arents. He was in daily conference at Moore & Schley's office with members of that firm, with Colonel Payne, and with Mr. Terrell. When they were ready, one day they called in Captain Duke and told him that he was deposed.

Mr. Duke is a person of some temper, and, in violation of the accepted rules of the game, he let his feelings get the better of him, which was probably well for him on this occasion. He made one leap into the center of the group and denounced the whole scheme. They had him in their grip so far as the captaincy was concerned; he knew that. But he could make a lot of trouble for that ship and probably scuttle her, and he vehemently swore he would do it. He said that he would not only throw overboard all the American Tobacco stock that he held (which would be exceedingly bad for those trying to put the price up to 200), but he would get a new ship of his own and compete in the cigarette business.

Perhaps his violence frightened somebody; perhaps there were more plottings involved than those of Keene. Anyway, Moore & Schley and Terrell and Payne cast in their lot with Captain Duke. At this unexpected turn of affairs, Keene surrendered the part of his scheme that contemplated the marooning of Duke and Arents, and a new bargain was struck that dealt only with the manipulating of the stock.

To this work Keene now turned his attention, intending to put the stock up to 200, and telling his friends that this was the opportunity of a lifetime, which it certainly seemed to be. But somehow the stock didn't go up. Mr. Keene chafed and fumed daily to Moore & Schley, and daily he was regaled with reasons. When his patience had been exhausted, he announced that he would put the stock up on his own account without anybody's assistance. Whereupon $3,100,000 of the common stock that was in the treasury of the American Tobacco Company was issued to Moore & Schley at 108¾, which was then the market price, and immediately and rapidly the stock was advanced until it reached 150!

But here another row broke out among the new associates.   Keene declared that some one in the Moore & Schley end of the combination was secretly selling his stock at 150 instead of holding it until it should reach 200, which was the agreement.   Of course so long as insiders let their stock go at 150, it was useless to talk of putting the thing above that figure.   Keene accused Moore & Schley and was in turn charged with treachery.   In the end Keene threw over the whole venture.   Within two days he sold all his tobacco stock for what he could get, from 147¾ down to 132½, clearing about $1,250,000, but missing the monstrous harvests that he had expected from the stock-watering.   He was out, but Payne and the Standard Oil crowd were in and stayed in, and that is where Standard Oil influence in the Tobacco Trust began.   Payne had snapped up most of Keene's stock.

But now the new crowd that surrounded Captain Duke turned back joyously to the original scheme of watering the stock.   The capitalization of American Tobacco was doubled.   Pretty soon it was still further increased.   The Continental Tobacco Company was organized and took in all the plug-tobacco manufacturers except Liggett & Myers, who absolutely refused to ship under Captain Duke. Various devices were adopted to swell still further the enormous capitalization without seeming to increase it, devices like the subsidiary company and the holding company. The American Snuff Company was formed to establish a monopoly in the snuff business, and the American Cigar Company to monopolize cigar-making. Every time the capital was increased, a heavier tribute was imposed upon retailer and consumer. After some years it occurred to the gentlemen in actual charge of the Trust that one source of profit had been overlooked, and thereafter the tobacco producer began to feel a steady contraction of his market and a decline of the prices that he obtained.

CHAPTER XI

THE SYNDICATE COMES IN

MEANTIME, Mr. Ryan and his friends had noted well the progress of the Tobacco Trust, and at the beginning of 1899 they seem to have thought that the time had come for them to participate in this good thing. Accordingly, and for purposes that will be more apparent as this narrative proceeds, they organized the Union Tobacco Company of New Jersey. Old friends of ours appear in the list of incorporators—Thomas F. Ryan, P. A. B. Widener, W. L. Elkins, Thomas Dolan, and R. A. C. Smith, and with gratification we may observe that the new enterprise had the sage advice and directing counsel of Elihu Root, now Secretary of State of this nation, then confidential adviser of Thomas F. Ryan.

The capital stock of the Union Tobacco Company was $10,000,000, of which, kindly note, only $1,350,000 was ever paid for. The news of its

forming occasioned many painful moments on
board Captain Duke's ship. The navigators there
easily foresaw trouble. Mr. Ryan and his friends
soon found the talent necessary to embark on a
large scale in the cigarette and tobacco business.
Among the experienced men that they secured was
William H. Butler, who had been vice-president
of the American Tobacco Company and the originator of the "Sweet Caporal" cigarette. It was
evident, therefore, that the Union Tobacco Company was equipped for formidable rivalry. Besides, the making and selling of tobacco was only a
part of the business of the American Tobacco Company. Manufacturing was a good cover to the
issuing and manipulating of securities from which
the bulk of the great profits was derived, and the
men in the Duke party knew very well that in the
issuing and manipulating of securities the Ryan-
Widener-Elkins-Root syndicate had no equals in
this world; also that to such experts $10,000,000
of capital was as good a foundation as $100,000,-
000. A still greater danger lay in the proved and
unequaled power of the Ryan party to influence
legislation and manipulate government—a matter
of the first importance to the Trust's welfare.

The first moves by the Union Tobacco Company

were very disconcerting. It had acquired the National Tobacco Company, a concern making a brand of cigarettes called the "Admiral"; it bought a majority of the stock of Blackwell's Durham Tobacco Company, of Durham, N. C., one of the firms that had remained outside of and had fought the Trust; and there were rumors that it was likely to take over or combine with the great Liggett & Myers institution.

These operations caused additional misery to Captain Duke and his friends. In the making of something out of nothing they had been enormously successful, and yet, it must be admitted, in a crude and blundering way. Opposed to them were men that had been all their lives engaged in making something from nothing and had shown in the process both finesse and industry. From the Duke ship the outlook seemed stormy indeed. Meanwhile the Ryan-Root syndicate proclaimed that it purposed to press resolutely ahead and to compete vigorously in every department of the tobacco trade. With hand upon heart, so to speak, it declared to the public that its one dear object was to combat monopoly. Before the agonized gaze of the retail trader, groaning and sweating under the screws of the Trust, the coming of the new com-

pany was a joy unspeakable. To the persecuted
consumer, who for some years had been noticing
a decline in the quality of his tobacco, there showed
at last a promise of relief and fair treatment. To
break the monopoly—that was the thing. Mr.
Ryan, Mr. Widener, and Mr. Root (whose sympa-
thies against monopoly in all its forms can be readily understood) bent themselves assiduously to this
congenial task. And this is how they did it. For
six months or less the gentlemen on Captain Duke's
quarter-deck looked into the muzzle of the pistol
held by the syndicate. Then they offered to surrender. What did the syndicate want? Well,
it wanted to be bought. For how much? For
$10,000,000 and a share in the control of the Trust
ship. That was all.

The terms were hard, but there was no other
way out of the situation. A battle with the syndicate would have sunk the ship and all on board.
There were too many and too big guns involved.
So the Duke party agreed to the terms. They
issued $35,000,000 of additional American To-
bacco stock, paid $10,000,000 of it for the paper-
fed Union Tobacco Company, bought the subsidiary
companies that the Union gentlemen had organized, and while Captain Duke still stood at the

wheel and issued orders, the new crowd studied the charts below and laid the course, and that new crowd was composed of Mr. Ryan and his friends.

Probably their most remarkable achievement was their performance with Liggett & Myers. The attempted Keene mutiny had revealed the fact that Liggett & Myers would join a combination, or sell to one, opposed to the American. The Ryan-Root-Widener syndicate (or some one in their interest), acting on this hint, made up a pool of $200,000 and with it secured an option for sixty days to purchase the Liggett & Myers business at $11,000,000. Before the sixty days expired the American had capitulated to the Union. Thereupon the syndicate compelled the American to purchase of it the Liggett & Myers business at $18,-000,000, thereby netting a profit of $6,800,000 on an expenditure of $200,000.

The profits of the syndicate in its Union Tobacco deal were stupendous. It put into the venture $1,350,000. Besides securing control of one of the greatest profit-makers in the world, the syndicate cleared on the Liggett & Myers deal $6,800,-000, on the sale of Union Tobacco Company $8,-650,000, and in operations in other concerns like the Blackwell Company probably $2,000,000 more, comprising a total of about $17,000,000.

This in less than six months, without making anything, selling anything, or developing anything; and also without effort, risk, or expenditure, except for options and for the issuing of fictitious stock.

Of the $35,000,000 of additional American stock, $21,000,000 went as another scrip dividend to the holders of American Tobacco, who were thus again presented with riches that represented nothing but the enforced contributions of the public.

No sooner was this pleasant affair concluded than the new directors of the ship began some dizzy evolutions on a broader sea.

You may recall that the subsidiary company organized to control the plug trade and fight Liggett & Myers had been called the Continental Tobacco concern. It was floated in New Jersey, December 9, 1898, with $75,000,000 capital stock, half common and half preferred, of which there was issued $31,145,000 of preferred and $31,146,500 of common. Its business was unsatisfactory because of the cost of fighting the firms still outside the Trust and because it was monstrously overcapitalzed to start with, so that its net earnings for 1899 were only $2,032,756, and it paid only three per cent. on the preferred and nothing on the common. It was with this branch of the business that the new control elected to work. The war with Spain had brought about greatly increased revenue duties on tobacco. After the war closed, the tobacco interests desired to have these duties reduced to a peace basis, but on the plea that the Government needed the money Congress had refused to make any reduction.

The new interests in the American Tobacco Company had very good friends in Washington, for one of the remarkable features of the Ryan syndicate is the close relations it has always managed to maintain with government—city, state, and national. Of its many friends in Washington the best seem to have been in and about the Finance Committee of the Senate, where all these matters of the revenue duties would be determined. Afterward it was learned that Senator Nelson W. Aldrich, of Rhode Island, held $1,000,000 of tobacco stock. Very likely, therefore, he was not among the deadly or implacable enemies of the Trust. Senator Aldrich was chairman of the Finance Committee. Two other members of the Senate were also holders of tobacco stock. Very likely, too, these gentlemen were not wholly inimical to the Trust.

In secret sessions the Finance Committee of the Senate determined to reduce the tobacco tax to the peace basis. It also determined to make in the revenue laws certain changes that would be greatly to the benefit of the Trust and to the disadvantage of the Trust's competitors. These were changes (difficult to make clear in this limited space) in the restrictions governing the sizes of packages, changes that had the effect of enabling the Trust to undersell makers of brands then on the market by offering larger packages for the same price.

Knowledge of these impending changes was kept a profound secret—except from the men that controlled the Trust.

Immediately these men went into the market and bought all the Continental stock they could find. When they began to buy it was quoted at 12 and was inert. Unluckily, the time was short and they had no chance to work the device by which a man buys while he pretends to sell, and thus keeps the price from rising. The gentlemen were compelled, for once, to buy outright, and after a time the stock began to feel the effects. The price rose to 17, 18, 20, 22—but not before, at bottom prices, the gentlemen had secured vast loads of it.

When this had been done, out came the news

from Washington that the revenue duties were to be reduced, and up bounded the prices of all tobacco stocks.

But the gentlemen that managed the Trust had secured theirs beforehand, and they now proceeded to reap the golden harvest, which amounted for them to about $15,000,000.

Meantime, the capital stock of the American Tobacco Company, which had been $25,000,000 in 1890, was nominally $68,500,000 in 1900, and with the subsidiary and other companies amounted to $200,000,000 and more.

With every desire to be temperate and fair, I am obliged to say that, so far as I can discover, the creating of this colossal something from nothing had involved no risk, no effort, little or no investment, no development of any industry, no economic equivalent, and no higher type of mentality than controls the simplest operation of the smallest country store.

Nor have we, by any means, seen the last of this easy fortune-making. In June, 1901, the gentlemen in control, under the pretense of extending to foreign and less favored lands the blessings of the trust principle, formed a new concern, the Consolidated Tobacco Company, and of course out came a new flood of water. The capital stock of the Consolidated Tobacco Company was $40,000,-000, and it issued $157,378,200 of four per cent. bonds, making its total capitalization nearly $200,-000,000. With these fresh tokens of something from nothing it took over the American and the Continental, giving $100 in four per cent. bonds for every $50 of American and $100 in four per cent. bonds for every $100 of Continental. The public tolerance being not yet exhausted, the same old game was worked again on these issues, and again the insiders, having knowledge of what was toward, picked up Continental stock in advance and added further millions to their vast hoards.

In pursuance of the decision to extend to our friends abroad the joys of a business thus conducted, the Trust now sailed for British waters. As to what happened there I think it best to summon a witness. I have found that to question in any way the ability, energy, and foresight of men that in a short time and by these methods accumulate great fortunes is fraught with some danger. It is attacking the most sacred doctrine of that commercial religion of which they are the high priests. I have an idea that the voyage of this American Trust to England was not a brilliant suc-

cess: I have something more than a suspicion that
the ship was badly handled and only by chance and
the dexterity of Mr. Ryan rescued from the hardy
bands of attacking Englishmen; but it would probably be sacrilege and impiety to say so. Everything
done by the leaders of our financial world must be
a success and must, if properly considered, reveal
to us anew how infinitely inferior are the rest of
us.

In *Frank Leslie's Popular Monthly* for March,
1903, there appeared an account of these matters.
that I understand has been approved by persons
high in authority in the Trust, so I have secured
permission to quote it here:

"A conflict that was brief in duration but decis-
ive and vastly important in its bearing upon the
tobacco trade of the world, was the struggle waged
during the past year and a half in the English market. This international war started in the year
1901, when the Americans bought Ogden's Limited, one of the best known of British tobacco
houses, and began a campaign of American methods
to push its goods.

"The British tobacco trade was thrown into great
excitement by this step. The Imperial Tobacco

Company was organized, taking in the leading English houses, and proceeded to fight the invaders.

"Intending to wipe out the Americans by a single master-stroke, the Imperial offered to divide one-fifth of its total profits among dealers not handling American goods, and in addition announced that $200,000 would be distributed among the dealers taking advantage of its offer within the first six months. Not to be outdone by his adversaries, Mr. Duke promptly announced that his company would distribute $1,000,000 per year for four years, and that all the profits of Ogden's for the same period would be divided among the dealers. Perhaps the most remarkable feature of Mr. Duke's royal offer was that it contained no stipulation as to the exclusive handling of his goods. He simply agreed to give $4,000,000 and all the profits of Ogden's for four years to the British tobacco dealers, irrespective of whether they handled the Imperial brands or not. England gasped at the daring of the move, for such methods of capturing trade had never been heard of there before.

"The rivals presently decided, however, that peace was more profitable than war. In the autumn of 1902 it was announced that an amicable agreement had been reached, by the terms of which each was to handle the goods of the other in its own territory, while the British-American Tobacco Company had been formed to handle the trade in foreign countries.   Mr. Duke gave a magnificent dinner to his associates and some of his late rivals and then sailed away for home.   The British press jubilantly announced that a crushing defeat had been administered to the Yankees, and that the latest American invasion had been a failure.

"As a matter of fact the terms of the peace treaty were as follows: The Imperial purchased Ogden's at Mr. Duke's own valuation and gave the Americans a large, though not a controlling interest, in their company.   It was also agreed that the Imperial should have the trade of Great Britain and Ireland to itself.   It was likewise arranged that the American company, in which of course the British had no interest, should remain in undisputed possession of the United States, Cuba and the Philippines.   To deal with the outside trade the British-American Tobacco Company was formed, with both English and American directors, but with the Americans in control.   In other words, the Imperial surrendered the entire foreign market to the

control of the Americans and gave them an interest
in its own business as the price of peace."

As to the activities elsewhere the same authority
says:

"In the field of the domestic-made Havana cigar
—that is, of cigars manufactured in the United
States from Havana tobacco—the Trust is represented by the Havana-American Company, which
secured a number of the factories at Tampa, which
is the chief seat of this industry. It also controls
the Havana Tobacco Company, with factories in
Havana, which supplies the bulk of the Cuban-
made Havana cigars imported into the United
States."

It will be seen, therefore, that the province of
this business is truly enormous.

But to return to our own affairs.

The Consolidated Tobacco Company was by no
means the last illustration of high finance that these
records afford. If I may be believed by the un-
initiated, the device that had been worked so often
to the injury of the public and the ruin of the retailer was employed again. On September 9, 1904,

there appeared a new American Tobacco Company, which, with another flood of water, took over the Consolidated, the Continental, the old American, and all the rest of the outfit, and again multiplied the capitalization on which the country must furnish the profits.

For instance, the new company retired the $157,-378,000 of the Consolidated Company's four per cent. bonds by giving one-half six per cent. preferred stock in the new company and one-half four per cent. bonds.   Six per cent. bonds were given for old American Tobacco preferred stock at the rate of 133⅓ a share, and for Continental preferred at 116⅝.   Besides all these securities the new company had $100,000,000 of common stock of its own, and in the year of grace 1906, on this stock thus made of nothing, it paid 22½ per cent. in dividends.

At the present time, the total capitalization of the whole enterprise, including the dummy, subsidiary, alias, assisting, and other companies is about $500,000,000, all created from $25,000,000 of speculative and paper assets put together by Captain Duke and his friends in 1890.

As an indication of how the thing has grown,

I quote figures from the American Tobacco Company alone, showing nine years' expansion:

Balance-Sheet Liabilities

	Dec. 31, 1897	Dec. 31, 1906
Preferred stock	$11,935,000	$78,689,100
Common stock	17,900,000	40,242,400
Scrip	3,762,340	....
Six per cent. bonds	....	55,208,350
Four per cent. bonds	....	61,052,100
Profit and loss surplus	7,447,849	30,353,888
All balance-sheet liabilities	42,289,236	278,628,564

Balance-Sheet Assets

Real estate, etc.	$4,009,143	....
Patents and good-will	24,867,263	$123,331,600
Leaf tobacco and manufacturing goods	8,591,777	31,187,814
Stock of foreign companies	1,264,655	21,495,085
Stock of other companies	....	70,451,549
Cash	1,538,751	5,163,965
Bills receivable	2,017,645	26,998,551

So stands this colossal and astounding structure erected upon the good-natured tolerance of the American people. The like successful exploitation has never been known in any land at any time. One of the men that have drawn golden fortunes from it, one that in 1890 was penniless and harassed with debts, now counts more than $40,000,000, made without labor, without effort, without investment, without risk, without the vestige of any return to society.

On the increasing mass of stocks and bonds, the issuing of which has occasioned this man's fortune, there have been paid, and are now being paid, great sums in dividends and interest charges.

Where do these dividends and interest charges come from and who pays them?

And now we reach the heart of the whole matter.

CHAPTER XII

THE TRUE DIMENSIONS OF A GREAT MONEY-MAKING MACHINE

I OFFER here for consideration two isolated facts:

1. At one o'clock on the morning of December 1, 1906, three hundred armed men rode into Princeton, Ky., seized the night-watch, locked up the town's fire apparatus, and proceeded to burn two tobacco warehouses reported to be owned by or connected with the Tobacco Trust.*

*I should observe here that in behalf of the American Tobacco Company it is urged that the company had no interest in these warehouses, and that the raiding and burning of tobacco warehouses that disturbed Kentucky in the winter of 1907-1908 were not directed against the company, nor a result of anything the company had done. One of the burned warehouses at Princeton, according to this statement, "belonged to an Irish manufacturer named Gallagher, and one of them belonged to the Imperial Tobacco Company." To judge of the full rich humor of this remark we must return to a foregoing page and reread the account of the division of the world's territory between the American and English interests. And then we may well recall such despatches as this, sent out by the Associated press:

LOUISVILLE, Jan. 9.—Militiamen left to-day for Lebanon to protect the property of the American Tobacco Company, which has been threatened by night-riders.

While the fires were under way the armed men were drawn up in lines of defense about them and prevented any attempt to extinguish the flames. As soon as the warehouses were destroyed, the men released the watch and the fire apparatus and rode away. Three hundred thousand pounds of tobacco had been burned.

The men engaged in this outbreak of violence were not bandits nor ruffians; they were peaceful farmers. They did not desire wantonly to destroy property; they had been goaded by what they regarded as extortions and fraud against which they had no protection, to revenge themselves in the only way in their power upon the men that had oppressed them.

2. In April, 1907, Hermann Beck, a well-known retail tobacconist of Portland, Ore., having lost his once flourishing business, committed suicide. He had lost his business because he had been driven out of it by the Tobacco Trust.

The first of these incidents illustrates what the Trust has done for the producer; the second, what it has done for the retailer. The two being multiplied and extended indicate where the money has come from that paid the dividends and interest on the watered American Tobacco securities.

The United Cigar Stores Company, a branch of the Trust, has more than 500 retail cigar stores in the country (183 of them in New York City), and speaking roughly, each of these represents a former retailer that has been deprived of his business. The method by which he has been deprived of it is one of the few operations of the Trust that have been visible to the eyes of the layman. It is a process that most observant persons must have seen or known of—the little independent dealer overpowered and crushed by the big Trust store next door—but few are aware, I suppose, of the tragedies that are sometimes involved in the crushing. Some of the crushed dealers have been old men, whose one source of livelihood lay in their little shops. Some have been Civil War veterans, some have been for many years in the one place and the one trade, some have been cripples and invalids. All have gone the one way when the Trust started to capture their businesses. Sometimes the Trust has resorted to extreme measures to pull them down. It has induced their landlords to raise their rent to unendurable figures; it has bought the property they rented; very often it has pushed them to ruin by giving tobacco away or selling at prices that made competition impossible. A certain dealer in Broadway, New York City, that has for years bravely resisted the Trust has been fought from two cigar stores adjoining him. For one of these the rental is $20,000 a year, which is said by one authority to be more than a year's total sales in that store. On the morning that this particular place opened, the man it was designed to crush walked into it and saw behind the counter four salesmen that had formerly been independent cigar dealers and had been driven out of business by the Trust. It was now using them to drive out others. Such as are young and active among the ruined tradesmen can usually find (for a time) employment with the Trust, employment at small salaries and under humiliating conditions. The older men shift for themselves or go to the poorhouse.

I do not know how many suicides like that of Hermann Beck have resulted from these operations. The remaining retailers say there have been many. Certainly Beck's is not the only case. The whole history of the development has been a story of cruel hardship. I will give one example.

Joseph Liebman kept for many years a cigar store at No. 264 West 125th Street, New York City. Agents of the Trust came to him about four years ago and told him that he had better retire from that neighborhood, as the Trust was about to open a store there. Liebman declined to move. The agent said that he would be crushed as other small dealers had been crushed before him. He replied that he had a good trade and plenty of strong friends and was not afraid of competition. The Trust opened a store next door. Liebman was undismayed. The Trust store began to give away cigars and tobacco. Liebman held on. Then the Trust leased the ground on which Liebman's store stood and bought the building. As soon as his term expired, the Trust put him into the street with his stock and fixtures, which he was obliged to place in storage until he could find quarters at No. 201 West 125th Street. Now he has to operate a barber's shop to make a living.

This is a typical case: wherever the Trust has appeared it has achieved similar triumphs; its pathway to success and profits has been over the ruins of the small tradesman's prosperity. On a certain stretch of Broadway where ten years ago were thirty-six independent cigar stores are now but six; and the former proprietors of the other thirty are either salesmen for the Trust, servitors, dependent for their bread upon whim, fancy, and caprice, subject to espionage and suspicion; or they have sought other work; or they have died.   And so the Trust has wrought everywhere.

As for the producer, that is a still more melancholy story.   From time immemorial in the tobacco-raising regions tobacco leaf had been sold at the free competition of buyers.   There was never any quoted price for tobacco as there is for wheat or cotton, but the farmers brought their tobacco to market and the buyers were wont to bid for it.   The Trust has changed all this, for now in a great part of the tobacco region there is but one buyer.   The Trust makes the price what it pleases, and the farmer must accept this price or take his tobacco home again.

Under the operation of this system, such tobacco as for years had brought in a free and open market six to eight cents a pound, sells for three cents a pound or less.   The land that had formerly produced $75 to $200 an acre now yields less than half of its former returns, and a distinguished Kentuckian has calculated that in his State, because of the operation of the Trust, the returns to the tobacco farmer are less than twenty cents a day for his labor.

In four of the countries of Europe—France, Italy, Austria, and Spain—tobacco is a government business, and these four governments buy in the United States every year about one million pounds of tobacco. It is denied that there has been any understanding between the Trust and the buyers for these governments by which competitive buying has been destroyed. Nevertheless, the same distinguished Kentuckian is responsible for the statement that the buyers for the governments now restrict themselves to certain territory where they buy without competition and that they keep out of the rest of the tobacco-growing region. Of course, those that understand the methods of the Trusts will hardly need to be told that such a condition might easily exist and still there might be no treaty, agreement nor understanding that could be adduced in court. The Trusts are not conducted by idiots. They have never been found butting their heads against the law when they can in other ways and safely get what they want.

Anyway, the departure of the government buyers destroyed the last chance of competition, and gave over the producer bound to his despoiler.

Against these conditions the farmers of the South have protested to Congress, to the Department of Commerce and Labor, and to the courts. Yet the law has never been enforced upon this Trust, nor has the government until lately given it any greater heed than is involved in some feeble, perfunctory, and quickly abandoned inquiries.

Meantime, there is the consumer, of whom nobody seems to think much.   What does it mean for him that competition has been eliminated, that the profits of the American Tobacco Company have been swollen to these stupendous figures, that the owners of the Trust are becoming the richest men in the world?

This is what it means for him:

The Trust has secured the ownership of many well-known brands of Havana, Key West and domestic cigars, brands that have been familiar for years upon years to all smokers and that for years upon years have maintained an even degree of excellence.   Many good judges of tobacco assert that under the names of these brands the Trust puts forth steadily a worse quality of goods, until at last the brand dies.   Their theory is that before its death the Trust has sold great quantities of the brand, these goods have been produced at perhaps one-third of the original cost, and the profits have been enormous.

So far has this work been carried that some of the brands of cigarettes and smoking tobaccos formerly best known have disappeared entirely from the market. Why should the Trust not do as it pleases in these matters? Every day the consumer finds greater difficulty in discovering a cigar store outside of the Trust; every day a greater proportion of the retail business is seized by the Trust. Many stores that pretend to be independent and do not fly the Trust flag, are really owned by the Trust; you can hardly tell when you are buying of the Trust and when you are not. Great, glittering, brilliantly lighted stores, cleverly worded advertisements, specious promises of low prices, attract and delude the consumer; it does not seem possible that bad goods can come from such imposing places. With much cunning the Trust has brought into the business the influence of women. Imitating the trading-stamp device, it holds forth bribes in the shape of coupons that are exchangeable for articles of household use, and thus it induces women to urge their husbands to buy at Trust stores. As the Trust, by the use of inferior tobacco, by making large purchases, and by robbing the producer, has an abnormal margin of profit, it can of course well afford these bribes.

So that here at last is displayed in the clearest colors the exact meaning and results of the Formula

for Wealth-making when that formula has done its
perfect work.   The bonds are issued, the stock is
floated, the syndicate is enriched, the palace arises.
And every cent thus represented we furnish: we
that consume the tobacco, ship the freight, grow
the crops, eat the beef, hang to the straps of the
street cars, pay for the bad gas, endure the bad
service; we upon whose backs is piled the whole
vast mass of watered stocks, fictitious bonds, fraudulent scrip, gambling securities.   And the only
profit obtained by society in all these operations is
the spectacle of five or six men accumulating great
fortunes, fortunes beyond computation, fortunes
for a few comprising the sum of available wealth
that should be for all.

Such are the facts.   Sorry and stained and
wretched, in the light of them, looks also this particular palace among the golden houses of the fortunate.   Built out of the enforced contributions of
the public, the sweat of the defrauded farmer, the
blood of the small dealer, what interest has mankind in the mounting millions that it represents?
Or wherein have we gained from its existence, we
whose unexampled patience renders all these things
possible?

CHAPTER XIII

THE GREAT GAME OF INSURANCE

ONE thing that Thomas F. Ryan must quickly have learned about the golden city of his dreams has impressed itself upon all other men that have tried to master the money mart.

In the golden city is boundless wealth, but the vast mass of it is not to be touched, handled, come by, nor spun upon the table of the Wall Street game.

At that game the playing is done with counters. All are counters—credits, stocks, bonds, notes, accounts, buildings, railroads. Of tangible gold to redeem the counters there is very little. True, the banks are enjoined by law to the keeping of certain reserves in cash, and, true, so long as these reserves endure one may at the banks get cash for his counters; but the law has requirements (stern though sometimes violated) about borrowing upon counters, the operation is not easy, and the proportion of cash to counters is infinitesimal. Yet sometimes for the greatest and most profitable plays at the table great quantities of ready cash are absolutely necessary.

Amid the desert sands of counters, counters, always counters, flows one stream of actual cash, pouring steadily into New York. Day upon day, week by week, month after month, it comes in a solid, incessant stream, to fall into fewer than a dozen coffers. To the great insurance companies, that is where it all goes, millions upon millions of cash, not counters, paid daily by the policy-holders all about the world. The three great insurance companies have total assets of approximately a billion dollars, and this is the only free, large, and unrestricted source of ready money in the country.

Hence the madness of the struggle to gain control of these golden streams, for which men have risked the penitentiary and their souls. Year after year, as the business of the insurance companies grew and the golden stream rolled, the utility of the assets increased until hardly any new industrial enterprise could be floated without recourse to the policy-holder's money. Naturally, then, the money kings were impelled to get possession of the stream and to turn it whither they pleased.

The control of the policy-holder's money was in each case vested in the finance committee of the insurance company. In each case, also, the finance committee of the insurance company was composed of the money king and his friends. Hence the policy-holder's money could be used at any time to further, finance, or float the private schemes and ventures of the money king, to the money king's profit and the policy-holder's peril.

This was one use of the golden stream. Incidentally, there grew up another game with these millions, played at a side table and with great gains to the players. It consisted of what is known as "side syndicates." The substance of the "side syndicate" is a transaction not to be deemed honest merely because it happened to be developed since the framing of the criminal code. The men that controlled the insurance companies were also interested secretly in certain firms or companies whose business was to deal in securities. As these men directed absolutely the operations of the finance committees, their practice was to have their firms buy securities at a low rate and immediately, through the finance committees, sell them at a very high rate to the insurance companies. In this easy manner it was possible to make two or three millions in a morning without the least effort or risk.

Much more than chance or opportunity was involved in these operations. The thing was systematized, it was reduced to a faultless process in which the financiers held every advantage. The very spirit of the times played into their hands, for the rapid development of industrial enterprises through the country created an imperative demand for increased capital, and the supplies of available capital came to be almost exclusively with these finance committees.

Suppose, for instance, some great industrial enterprise in the booming Middle West desired to increase its facilities and extend its operations. It issued securities to the desired amount, and to dispose of them came straightway to New York—the financial capital of the Western World and supposedly the only source of available cash. But once here in this financial capital the supporters of the Western enterprise found themselves confronting a strange difficulty. As a rule only a few, a very few, specified firms or bond companies would handle their issue. Of these there was a regular list perfectly well known. When after negotiation one of these firms agreed to undertake the issue it was always at a price distinctly below the price that in view of the state of its market might reasonably have been expected. But the firm that purchased the bonds did not keep them. It transferred them at a much greater price to an insurance company whose finance committee had probably refused to take the same bonds at a lower price from the company that issued them.

The real point of this transaction was that the gentlemen that controlled the finance committee also controlled the firm that handled the bonds. In other words, what happened was that in their own capacity they bought the bonds at 80 and then in their capacity as finance committee sold them to the insurance company at 90, thereby safely and rapidly drawing the money from the policy-holders' pockets into their own.

The absolute security of this artless method of getting It was enhanced by the conditions of the insurance business. Nobody outside of a little coterie in each of the great companies had any idea of the true nature of the business transacted. The policy-holder knew that the company was perfectly solvent, which was true; that it had enormous and increasing assets and reserves; that in the event of his death his heirs were absolutely certain to re-

ceive the amount of his policy.   What he did not
know was that he was not deriving his share of the
company's prosperity; that he was paying more for
his insurance than the conditions warranted; and
that from lapsed policies, fortunate investments and
the inevitable accumulative force of great capital
there were gathered huge sums that should have
been applied to the reduction of his premiums, but
were in fact applied for the private advantage of
the gentlemen that managed the company.

What was still more curious in this strange chapter in the history of human credulity was that in
most instances these same gentlemen had no possible rights over the money they manipulated, but
merely represented the policy-holders to whom
alone the money belonged.   This is, of course,
morally and essentially true in the case of every
insurance company that invites men to entrust it
with their funds; but it was peculiarly and strikingly
true in the case of two of the great companies, for
these were organized strictly upon the mutual plan
and had no owners except the policy-holders.

For years upon years the money of these policy-
holders was squandered and used for the personal
benefit of the men that managed it; it was wasted
in idle attempts to make surpassing showings of new

business acquired; it was wasted on dinners, banquets and the bribery of legislatures and politicians; it was wasted in small varieties of "graft" and in great.

Meantime the patient policy-holder continued to know naught about the important subject of his life insurance except that his premiums remained the same, year after year, and that the business assets and resources of his company steadily mounted. But all unknown to him there were mounting also the private fortunes of the manipulators made from the patient policy-holders' assets.

Shall we remind ourselves of what happened next? One of these merry gentlemen gave a dinner (with the policy-holders' assets) to a French actress. The patient policy-holder took note of the fact. Some of the merry gentlemen began to quarrel among themselves over the criticisms that followed and to reveal in their quarreling the exact nature of the profits they were drawing from the patient policy-holder. The patient policy-holder reached the end of a patience that the financial world confidently believed had no limit. He began to demand his own. A committee was appointed by the State Senate to investigate these matters. Scratching with anxious care to disturb only the surface and avoiding all the most important matters, this committee nevertheless disclosed a state of things that struck the entire country breathless, for through all the fog and verbiage there appeared the fact that from the systematic and incessant plucking of the patient policy-holder year after year the gentlemen were feathering their nests.

In other words, as so often happens in modern business, it appeared that insurance was only a blind for other and more profitable transactions, just as carrying passengers in Chicago was a blind for the stock juggling of Mr. Yerkes, and the State Trust Company was a blind for office-boy loans.

This is the game, as to a certain degree it was revealed by the insurance investigation of 1905, which we have all happily forgotten. It went on for years, it is going on now, it will always go on until we come to our senses in regard to the conduct of our insurance business.

The Standard Oil Company's able financiers had long been interested in the insurance business as thus carried on in New York. So had been Mr. Morgan. Mr. Ryan closely followed Mr. Morgan's course, and frequently came in to share the proceeds of the Morgan operations. Mr. Rogers controlled the Mutual, Mr. Morgan controlled the New York Life, and other colossal interests manipulated the Equitable, all to the same purpose of catching the golden stream and sending it where it would do the most good—for the personal fortunes of the manipulators.

No man had more schemes that needed financing than Mr. Ryan; his vast and complicated enterprises in traction, tobacco, railroads, mines, and the Congo, insistently demanded capital. There were the insurance assets as the great available source of ready capital, and Mr. Morgan and Mr. Rogers were in chief control of the supplies. But the three big insurance companies were not the only insurance companies in New York; there were others, not so conspicuous, but with some share in the golden stream. In January, 1905, Wall Street was deeply interested to learn that in the preceding November Mr. Ryan had quietly secured control of the Washington Life-Insurance Company and was then engaged in reorganizing it on a plan of his own. It was in a way a small concern, with a capital stock of only $125,000, which Mr. Ryan (quite consistently) increased to $500,000; but it had assets of $17,000,000, and there was presently reason to believe that these were not without their uses.

Mr. Ryan brought over Mr. John Tatlock to be president of his reorganized company. Mr. Tatlock had been for many years an actuary of the Mutual Life, and secured leave of absence to take his new position—a fact that shows the ramifications of the ties that firmly bind together the interests of the dominating forces in our affairs. Mr. Ryan's influence in the Mutual was secured through the Morton Trust Company, which he owns, and which is and long has been one of the side operators for the great insurance company.

Mr. Tatlock was a witness before the Armstrong investigating committee in December, 1905, and, examined by Mr. Hughes, he gave some extremely interesting testimony. It appears that when Mr. Ryan took control of the company in November, 1904, it had $453,000 of its assets invested in securities and $6,300,000 in real estate. From January 1, 1905, to the time when the witness was testifying, $4,000,000 of the assets had been invested in securities, and the real-estate investments had been reduced by $2,000,000, some of the loans on real estate being called—presumably to effect the investments in securities. Mr. Tatlock said that among the securities the company had bought were:

American Tobacco bonds.

Seaboard Air Line bonds.

Atlantic Coast Line bonds.

Second Avenue Railroad bonds.

Westchester Lighting Company bonds.

Brooklyn City Railroad bonds.

American Tobacco stock.

All these are enterprises of the Whitney-Ryan syndicate and its allies.

These securities were purchased through the firm of Ryan & Kelly, of which Mr. Ryan's son was the senior member.

Mr. Hughes also brought out the fact that the auditing committee of the insurance company had taken alarm at some of these purchases of the finance committee, and had said that the State Superintendent of Insurance would not approve of them. It advised that no more securities of the kind be purchased, and thereupon some of the securities had been sold—also through Ryan & Kelly.

The finance committee of the company, which directed the handling of the assets, was composed of Mr. Ryan, Mr. Tatlock, and Mr. Levi P. Morton.

Mr. Tatlock also admitted that, since the reorganization of the company, it had become a depositor at the National Bank of Commerce of New

York, a Ryan concern, and that its account with Mr. Ryan's Morton Trust Company had been doubled. Which will sufficiently indicate the channels that the assets were taking.

Further, Mr. Tatlock admitted that, since the company's reorganization, it had participated in six of these "side syndicate" deals, although the company had never before been engaged in such enterprises. It appeared further that these syndicates were in the kind of industrial securities that the auditing committee had condemned. When Mr. Hughes called Mr. Tatlock's attention to this singular fact, Mr. Tatlock merely said:

"I had my instructions."

So the situation seems to be reasonably clear so far as the Washington Life is concerned.

But in the mean time Mr. Ryan had startled the entire world by another move of far greater magnitude. On June 15, 1905, it was announced that the months of scandal and bickering in the great Equitable Company had come to an end because Mr. Ryan had bought of Mr. James Hazen Hyde the controlling interest (502 shares) in the Equitable stock that Mr. Hyde had inherited from his father. It had been supposed that the elder Hyde had so tied up this stock that its sale was impos-

sible.   Repeatedly the younger Hyde had refused
on any terms to part with it.   Only a few days before he had rejected an offer for it, from Mr. E. H.
Harriman, of $5,000,000.   And now he had sold
it to Mr. Ryan for $2,500,000.   So ran the report;
Mr. Hyde would not deny it.   The Street was
amazed.   What had induced Mr. Hyde to change
his mind in this extraordinary fashion?   There
were a thousand surmises.   Mr. Ryan was supposed to have hypnotized the young man, or to have
obtained over him some sinister control; but the
silent Ryan heard all and gave no sign.

Only one thing seemed perfectly certain: the
Equitable and its vast assets, its steady stream of
gold, its huge power upon business, the drag of its
millions, and their bewildering possibilities of profit-
making, lay in Mr. Ryan's hands.   In the other
companies the policy-holders may some day weary
of furnishing money for the Wall Street game and
may kick over the table at which the Standard Oil
gang and Mr. Morgan now sit at ease.   In the
Equitable (since it is a stock company) there can
hardly be a revolt.   Mr. Ryan controls it, he has it
in his vest-pocket, he can do with it as he may
please, the "side syndicates" may produce untold

millions, the assets may be used in any undesirable way—the policy-holders will have little to say.*

When he was a witness before the Armstrong Committee, Mr. Ryan was asked what were the motives that induced him to buy the Equitable. Mr. Hughes put the question.

Mr. Ryan replied that his motives were purely philanthropic. I regret to say that on the publication of this reply, Wall Street, which ordinarily has no sense of humor, gave vent to cynic laughter, possibly thereby doing injustice to Mr. Ryan.

"I thought," he said, "I was doing a great public service, and preventing what I feared would be

---

*This remains practically true in spite of what is called the "mutualization" of the company by which the policy-holders are allowed to name a majority of the directors. The easy manner in which the gentlemen behind the scene can control the actual choice of any such body was abundantly shown in the so-called "elections" held in the Mutual and New York companies in the autumn of 1906. The policy-holders were supposed in these elections to name not only a majority but all of the directors or trustees, and the result was that in each case the board selected was composed entirely of friends or creatures of the gentlemen behind the scenes. The device of allowing the Equitable policy-holders to name a majority of the directors is therefore very shallow. The actual control of these companies is just as much in the hands of the money kings as it ever was. No matter how much the policy-holders may be allowed to play at casting votes, the control will remain with the money kings until we weary at last of allowing the momentous matter of life insurance to be the plaything of private greed.

the most tremendous panic this country has ever seen, if the Equitable Life-Assurance Society had gone into the hands of a receiver."

The Equitable was then carrying $6,500,000 of Mr. Ryan's Metropolitan Street-Railway stock. At the recollection of this fact Wall Street laughed again.

And yet, I think that when Mr. Ryan said that he had bought Mr. Hyde's interest in the Equitable, he must have used the word in a sense not recognized by lexicographers, because, according to expert authority, he had not bought it at all. How easily we are all fooled! The mystery of Mr. Hyde's sale for $2,500,000 of stock worth $7,500,000 was really no mystery. Mr. Ryan knew well enough the potentialities of the Equitable assets; Mr. Hyde probably perceived that there would be bickering so long as he remained ostensibly in control. Hence Mr. Ryan easily induced him to lease the stock, and that is the arrangement now in force. Mr. Hyde remains the owner.

But for the purposes of the game a lease of the stock is as good as a purchase, and it is pleasing to know that with Mr. Ryan in control of the Equitable, the Standard Oil gang of the Mutual, and Mr. Morgan of the New York Life, the good old game does prosper and go merrily, and no mistake. Every day you can hear in Wall Street the clink of the policy-holders' dollars as they roll over the table, making profits for the deserving "System," and for others in authority over us, just as if the names of Armstrong and Hughes had never been heard in this world.   Wonderful are the achievements of a legislative investigation!   The net results of our virtuous indignation about the insurance scandals are a few men worried to death, two or three in exile, two obscure persons sentenced to prison, and the game exactly as before.

Great thing, this spasmodic indignation of ours.

Mr. Ryan chose for president of his share in the game Secretary of the Navy Paul Morton, formerly of the Atchison, Topeka & Santa Fé Railroad, and involved in very serious charges of having violated the anti-rebate law.   There is no reason to suppose that Mr. Morton and Mr. Elihu Root ever compare notes as to their respective careers, but such a comparison, now that both are working for Mr. Ryan, might prove mighty interesting.

CHAPTER XIV

THE WRECK OF A GREAT PROPERTY

On October 8, 1907, a quiet little man was sitting in the witness-chair before the New York Public Service Commission, telling in a quiet little way some of the historic secrets of the Ryan-Whitney syndicate.

Much of his testimony was well worth the world's serious attention.

He admitted an instance of his own knowledge in which the syndicate had possessed itself of more than half a million dollars of the Metropolitan's money. How? Well, there was a so-called company with a so-called franchise to operate a so-called railroad between Wall Street Ferry and Cortlandt Street Ferry. Mr. Anthony N. Brady, the quiet little witness, owned this precious device. He said it cost him $200,000. Under the coercion of the syndicate, he sold it to the Metropolitan Securities Company, acting for the Metropolitan

Street-Railway Company of New York, then the name of the street railroads amalgamated by the syndicate. He received a check for $965,607.19. Of this he retained $250,000. Then by agreement he gave of the remainder, $111,652.27 to Thomas Fortune Ryan, $111,652.78 to William C. Whitney, $111,652.78 to P. A. B. Widener, $111,652.78 to Thomas F. Dolan, $111,652.78 to W. L. Elkins.

So here was a plain revelation of where some of the gentlemen had gotten It.

Every person that heard this cool recital, nearly every person that the next day read of it, was astounded. The whole country seemed to receive a kind of electric shock. Yet the really amazing thing was that there should have been any amazement. Any one that cared to know, any public prosecutor, for instance, or any State officer or newspaper editor, could have found out long ago, and with the greatest ease, not only the whole story of the Wall and Cortlandt streets railroad deal, but other matters, compared with which the Wall and Cortlandt streets railroad deal was mere child's play—in the way of loot.

As the evisceration of the Metropolitan Company was the crowning triumph of the syndicate's

achievements, and typical of all, and as it, moreover, presents the best possible illustration of exactly what these achievements mean for the public,
I purpose here to relate it at length, and without
comment, as the most instructive chapter in the history of modern finance.

On October 8, 1907, Judge Lacombe, in the
United States Circuit Court, acting on a petition
of certain stockholders, appointed receivers for
the New York City Railway Company, which
meant the Interurban Street-Railway Company,
which meant the Metropolitan Street-Railway
Company, which meant the vást system of surface
railroads amalgamated, unified, and controlled by
the Ryan-Whitney syndicate.

Ordinarily the appointment of a receiver for a
property has only one meaning. It means that the
property is depleted, impaired, unable to earn its
interest charges, and on the verge of bankruptcy.
But this great traction system of New York, this
wonderful money-earner, this inexhaustible hopper
into which so many thousands of people daily pour
their nickels, this concern once regarded as the Gib-
raltar of traction companies, whose stock was once
quoted at 269, how did it fall into a depleted and
bankrupt condition? Its business has not declined,

but increased; its expenses have not multiplied, but relatively diminished. It transports passengers for a five-cent fare each, and the average cost of transporting each passenger is two cents or less. What has become of the other three cents?

This is the question on which the whole subject revolves. Here is the answer to it:

When the syndicate first came into the New York field with the purchase of the old Broadway line, about twenty separate companies possessed the street-railroad business of the city. Eight main trunk lines ran north and south, or lengthwise of Manhattan Island; twelve or thirteen smaller lines crossed the city east and west. These, one after another, and year after year, the syndicate absorbed. Its impelling reason was then announced to be a desire to unify and improve the system. There is ground now to believe that the real motive was very different. Every absorption was accompanied by a new issue of securities, in the manipulation and disposal of which lay enormous profits. Sometimes the acquisition was by lease, and in such cases the stockholders of the added lines were induced to favor the lease because of the great dividends to be guaranteed on their stock, seven, eight, even ten per cent. Sometimes the absorption was

by purchase (so called), the operation being merely
the application of Mr. Yerkes's original Formula,
or, as it has since been called, the endless chain.
That is to say, having possession of one road, the
syndicate issued more securities upon it, and with
these securities purchased another road, with which
it repeated the simple operation.

But here some things are to be noted particularly.
First, in certain instances, the syndicate did not
merely buy the road in the name of the Metropolitan and directly from the company that owned the
property. The syndicate, acting for itself, purchased the road at a low price and then sold it at a
very high price from itself as the syndicate to the
Metropolitan Company, thus securing very great
profits for itself, but loading the Metropolitan with
a further weight of securities. Thus, the syndicate
bought the old Thirty-fourth Street Railroad—
about one-half mile in length, value about $100,-
000—issued upon it $2,000,000 of stocks and
bonds, and compelled the Metropolitan to purchase
the securities at par. In the same way it secured
the Twenty-eighth and Twenty-ninth Street lines
—value about $250,000—issued upon them $3,-
000,000 of securities, and then compelled the Metropolitan to purchase these securities also at par.

On these two transactions the syndicate cleared, without investment, and without effort, $4,650,000, and increased the capitalization $5,000,000.

Second, it is to be noted that all the roads acquired, whether by lease or by this system of purchase through the syndicate, were already heavily overcapitalized, and their acquisition was made the occasion for still further stock issues, so that what was bad anyway was made much worse, and the whole Metropolitan system began to be loaded with securities far beyond the support of its earning power. In some instances, the roads thus added at so great an expense were not profitable enterprises. Thus the Fulton Street road, which cost the Metropolitan $2,000,000, loses $25,000 a year, the Twenty-eighth and Twenty-ninth Street lines have never paid their operating expenses, and others are of a like nature.

The question that at once arises is why anyone should desire to injure one's own possessions.

The answer lies in the fact that in all of these operations the real profit has been, not in the operating of the property, but in the manipulating of the securities. Dividends were always a trifling thing compared with these profits, and the success of manipulating depended in no way upon the physical condition of the enterprise. It was practically as easy to float bonds on worthless old scrap-iron as upon a well-ordered and sound railroad. To the public mind a magical charm seemed to surround the Metropolitan. Whatever it had to offer must have value, for was it not the greatest street railroad in the world, with the most brilliant and certain future? Mr. Yerkes had made his millions by taking advantage of a similar situation in Chicago; other expert manipulators had similarly made millions elsewhere. Dividends! What were the slow and despised process of the dividend compared with the easy strokes of bond issuing that in a day gathered a monstrous fortune?

In the case of the Metropolitan and the syndicate there was also another still more stupendous source of gain, now to be explained.

In a foregoing chapter I mentioned the fact that from one operation in the securities of one subsidiary line, the Houston, West Street & Pavonia Ferry, the syndicate cleared $6,000,000. This was the manner of that transaction:

The Houston, West Street & Pavonia Ferry Railroad Company (so called) operated some crosstown and important East-Side lines. On October 1, 1890, it issued $6,000,000 of second-mortgage bonds. On June 17, 1893, the same company applied to the State Railroad Commissioners for permission to issue $6,000,000 of additional stock, for which the $6,000,000 of bonds issued in 1890 were to be exchanged. In the application the statement was made under oath that the bonds "had been issued and disposed of for sums of money necessary for completing, furnishing, or operating the railroads of your petitioner."

Please note:

1. None of the company's railroads had been "completed" or "furnished" in that time, and the paying of operating expenses from the proceeds would have been illegal, and would also have shown in the company's annual report, which reveals no such matter. There were no extensive repairs nor alterations upon any of the company's lines.

2. As a matter of fact, the $6,000,000 of bonds had not been used for any such purpose as was alleged, but had been exchanged for Metropolitan stock, an illegal transaction.

3. The bonds were issued October 1, 1890. The law required that they should be recorded in the company's annual report. The company's annual reports for 1890, 1891, 1892, 1893, do not mention them. These reports must be sworn to as cor-

rect. They were not correct, because the item of $6,000,000 of bonds was omitted. Hence the offi-cers that swore to the reports were guilty of per-jury, and, in a State where the laws are enforced, would have been sent to jail.

But here was $6,000,000 of stock issued to take up the bonds. Where were the bonds? Exchanged for Metropolitan stock. So that the $6,000,000 of stock was merely a cover for $6,000,000 of bonds that had disappeared. "Who got the money?" asked a Wall Street journal, commenting dazedly upon this wondrous performance. It might well ask. Not the stockholders at large, certainly; not the public, not the road. To the doors of the syndicate it was traced. Beyond that golden portal it vanished.

Who got the money?

CHAPTER XV

THE FATHOMLESS MYSTERIES OF HIGH FINANCE

BUT the cream of all these operations of thrift grew out of the work of "changing the motive power" of the roads from horse to electric. New York City, in its street railroad service, had been far behind most other great American communities. Electricity, which by 1890 had been introduced almost everywhere else, was still unused in New York as late as 1893. One reason for this was the unconquerable determination of the people not to allow their streets to be disfigured with the poles necessary for the overhead trolley system, and the absence of any other device for car propulsion. More than once a street railroad company approached the Board of Aldermen with a proposal to install the overhead system, but on every such occasion the storm of public wrath and the keen memory of the Jake Sharp scandal, frightened the aldermen from granting the necessary permits. On the Broadway, Third Avenue, and another line, the cable system, the early dream of William C. Whitney and Charles P. Shaw (an endless iron rope drawn over pulleys in an underground conduit between the tracks), was substituted for horse-power; but this system, while economical, was clumsy, inefficient, and unsatisfactory.

But meanwhile some Hungarian genius hit upon the idea of the underground electric trolley; the street railroads of Buda-Pest were operated successfully with this device; and in 1894 the syndicate adopted it, ostensibly for the entire Metropolitan system.

To put it into operation required the reconstructing of tracks and roadbed, the building (in some instances) of power houses, and the installing of electrical machinery. This is the process to which I refer now as "changing the motive power."

Among the important north and south roads acquired by the syndicate was the Second Avenue, with tracks from Fulton Ferry to Harlem River, and some branches. In 1898 this company issued $7,000,000 of bonds, whereof $1,960,000 were declared to be needed to meet certain obligations, and the remainder, $5,040,000, to pay for "changing the motive power" of the entire road.

Up to the present hour the motive power has been changed on one-half of the road. The rest continues to be operated with horses.

According to the company's reports, the amount of money expended in changing the motive power and installing electrical equipment (on twelve and three-quarters miles in a total of twenty-seven and three-quarters) was $1,933,171.47. All of this work was done, and all of this money was expended, in 1898. Since that date nothing has been done to change the motive power on any of the company's lines.

Yet in its report for 1900 the company declares that it expended in that year for changing the motive power $4,329,390.02, whereas no such sum was expended, and no work of changing the motive power was done.

Of the bonds issued for these improvements, $4,450,000 worth were sold. Of the money thus obtained, $1,933,171.47 was expended for the purpose designated when the bonds were issued. The difference between the real expenditure and the pretended expenditure was $2,396,218.55. This sum has disappeared.

Who got the money?

The report for 1902 of the Thirty-fourth Street

Railroad (part of the Metropolitan system) shows an expenditure of $245,435.63 for laying new rails in Thirty-fourth Street, between Lexington Avenue and Broadway.

The reports of the same company for 1903 and 1904 show an expenditure of $51,347.64 for the same purpose, making a total expenditure on this account of $296,783.27.

The exact length of track thus relaid was .48 of a mile. The rails used weighed 113 pounds to the yard, and cost $36 a ton. To lay .48 of a mile with such rails would cost $6,138 for the rails. Hence the company's reports would have us believe that the remainder of the item, $290,645.27, was spent for labor.

But the labor required consisted of tearing up the old rails and laying the new, and the true cost of this work was not $290,645.27, but less than $15,000.

How is this known? Very simply and surely.

In its report for 1902 the Central Cross-town Railroad (at that time an independent concern, with its own directorate and management) gave the cost of taking up four tracks in Fourteenth Street and relaying them with heavier rails as $10,-881.29 for the labor. The distance in Fourteenth

Street, from University Place to Seventh Avenue, is twenty-three feet shorter than the distance in Thirty-fourth Street, from Broadway to Lexington Avenue. The rails used in Fourteenth Street weighed 110 pounds to the yard; those used in Thirty-fourth Street weighed 113 pounds to the yard. Hence it is clear that the cost of the labor in these two instances was about the same. There was charged on the books of the Thirty-fourth Street company an expenditure of $290,645.27 for labor; there was actually expended for labor perhaps $12,000. A balance of $278,000 seems to have disappeared.

Who got the money?

In 1902 the syndicate determined to "change the motive power" on the Thirty-fourth Street line. On March 11th the chief engineer made a sworn statement in which he declared the cost of this change on this line to be $150,000, including power-house equipment and all other expenditures involved.

On June 30, 1902, three months and nineteen days later, the Thirty-fourth Street Railroad reported the expenditures made up to that date for changing the motive power to have been $831,-224.04.

The next year it changed more motive power

at a cost of $7,789.25, and the next year still more, at a cost of $228,970.91, making a grand total of $1,067,984.20 for changes in the motive power that the chief engineer swore could be effected for $150,000. Suppose his figures to have been too small by half, there would still remain more than $700,000 that disappeared under this item.

Who got the money?

On the Twenty-third Street cross-town line (North River to East River) the motive power has been changed four times in four years, if we are to believe the books and the reports. Thus there appear the following items:

```
1899—For changing motive power...............$1,100,932.52
1900—For changing motive power..............    362,424.38
1901—For changing motive power..............    373,401.64
1902—For changing motive power..............    225,470.74
                                              _____
      Total  ...................................$2,062,229.28
```

Distance, less than two miles; grade, level; work, easy.

This surpasses all the records of railroad construction in this or any other country. According to the reports, the work proceeded at the rate of half a mile a year, and required four years to complete. The cost of the work was at the rate of

$1,000,000 a mile, which is about the cost of boring a mountain tunnel. The average cost of surface railroad construction and equipment in this country is about $22,000 a mile. In Twenty-third Street the work seems to have cost $1,000,000 a mile. When the Second Avenue line was rebuilt and the motive power was changed, the cost was at the rate of $330,000 a mile of double track, including power-houses and equipment. At that rate the actual cost of changing the motive power in Twenty-third Street was about $600,000. There was charged for it $2,062,229.28. More than $1,400,-000 seems to have disappeared under this item.

Who got the money?

One of the cross-town lines acquired by the Metropolitan was called the Central Park, North & East River Railroad.

In the report of the State Railroad Commissioners for 1900 this company is charged with the cost of changing the motive power on its lines in First Avenue, from Thirty-fourth Street to Forty-second Street. In the report for 1901 there appears another item for the same charge, and in the report for 1902 still another item for the same charge. It appears, however, that this work had already been done and paid for by another of the subsidiary companies of the Metropolitan. The amounts that thus seem to have been wrongfully charged total $1,500,000.

Who got the money?

The book-keeping of the whole establishment seems to have been of the most extraordinary nature, and well deserving judicial inquiry. "Man is a cooking animal," says Charles Reade; "bankrupt man especially." If there has not been some fine culinary work in the kitchens of the Metropolitan, all the odors thence wafted are very deceptive. For instance, in the case of this same Central Park, North & East River Railroad here is a matter that seems plainly to indicate a most undesirable kind of cooking.

In the report of 1902 this company charged for the expenses of Engineering and Superintendence $322,340.45.

Now the total of the same expenses for the few years from 1899 to 1902 had been $341,731.39.

In those years the company had changed its motive power (in fact and not merely on paper) over a mile and one-half of its line; that is, in Fifty-ninth Street, from First Avenue to Tenth Avenue.

Taking as a basis the actual and ascertained cost of such changes, it appears that the amounts charged by this company for "Engineering and Superintendence" alone were almost sufficient to pay for the entire work of changing the motive power on the one and one-half miles of line, including also the cost of equipment. It seems likely that the actual cost of "Engineering and Superintendence" was not more than $1,500.

Some public comment was aroused by this discrepancy, and in the annual report of the Metropolitan, issued June 30, 1903, an attempt was made to forestall any further criticism, for there appears this item:

"Correction of error in 1902, in charging Track and Roadway and Electric Line Construction to Engineering and Superintendence, $262,787.90."

This, of course, shifted the charge from one account to another.

But it did not explain what had become of the money.

Yes, there must certainly be master cooks in the Metropolitan kitchen. As observe this further specimen of their art:

The New York Stock Exchange has a rule that a company seeking to list new securities must file with the Governors a sworn statement of its condition.

In May, 1904, the Metropolitan Company desired to list on the Stock Exchange a fine lot of newly watered bonds, fresh, and just out of its prolific garden. So it filed the required statement. It contained one very curious item, to wit:

"Fourteen thousand shares of Broadway & Seventh Avenue R. R. stock and National Cable Construction Company license right and privileges, $5,522,015.32."

Now, of course, these two items had no possible right to be amalgamated, because the Broadway & Seventh Avenue stock could have no connection with the Cable Construction Company's license. But beyond even that, here was the curious fact that the value of the Cable Construction Company's license and privileges was absolutely nothing. These things consisted of a permit to build a cable railroad. But a permit to build a cable railroad is worth nothing in New York, for the cable as a motive power has been long and forever abandoned. Hence here was something seemingly dishonest.

The value of 14,000 shares of Broadway & Seventh Avenue stock was at that time about $2,800,000.

It appears, therefore, that the cooks of the Metropolitan tried to show the assets of the concern to be $2,722,000 greater than they really were.

But these were by no means the only triumphs of those capable artists.

Thus in 1901 the Metropolitan reported this item: "Amount due from Lessor Companies June 30th, 1901, $2,245,598.78."

The next year, 1902, this item reappears as follows: "Balance due from Lessor Companies June 30th, 1901, $5,245,598.78."

In other words, in one year the same item had been swollen $3,000,000. In a region wholly given up to expert manipulation we shall always expect many instances of rapid and abnormal development. But no system of manipulation would seem to account for an item that one year is $2,245,598.78, and the next year becomes exactly $3,000,000 greater.

Sometimes the sum that disappeared was small, and sometimes it was large, but, large or small, it seemed to vanish and leave no trace.

On August 10, 1898, the Metropolitan Company applied for permission to increase its capital stock by $15,000,000. The sworn statement of President Vreeland, accompanying the application, declared that the money was to be used for these purposes:

To redeem $6,000,000 of debenture bonds...........$6,000,000
To pay for power-house construction and cars...... 4,000,000
To be held in the treasury and used when needed to
  complete the change of motive power on the various railroads owned and operated by the company. 5,000,000

Total $15,000,000

The chief engineer accompanied the application with an affidavit giving details of the proposed expenditures, from which it appeared that the Ninety-sixth Street power-house would cost, when completed, $2,975,580; the Fiftieth Street power-house, $600,000; and the new cars, $800,000, or a total of $4,375,580.

On the basis of the chief engineer's figures, there would be left from the proceeds of the stock sale $4,624,420, and, on the basis of Mr. Vreeland's figures, $5,000,000, to complete the change of motive power on the railroads owned and operated by the company.

But on June 28, 1900, the company applied for permission to issue still more stock, $7,000,000, and in this application President Vreeland said that $3,000,000 of the sum would be required to change the motive power on the company's own lines as distinguished from its leased lines. The chief engineer again put in his figures, and showed that the cost of changing the motive power on these owned lines would be $2,867,808. Adding to these the expenditures the chief engineer detailed with the application of 1898, it appears that the total cost of changing the motive power on owned lines and on leased lines was $7,243,386. Yet the company's report for 1902 declared that there had been expended for changing the motive power on owned and leased lines $13,310,977.87. The sum of $6,067,641.87 seems to have disappeared behind this item.

Who got the money?

Again, in the last six months of 1901 the Metropolitan Company borrowed $7,240,263.33 for new construction, and according to its report it expended for this new construction $6,900,494.26.

But there was no new construction in those six months, except what was involved in the changing of the motive power on a small part of the leased lines. The change of motive power on the company's own lines was provided for by the issues of additional stock already related.

Yet the report of the company asserts that in the

year 1901 there was expended for new construction $8,543,736.39, a sum large enough, according
to the figures of the chief engineer, to pay for changing the motive power on fifty-seven miles of railroad. As a matter of fact, for the year the company's actual expenditures upon new construction
were $2,105,195.10. The sum of $6,438,541.29
seems to have disappeared behind this item.

Who got the money?

CHAPTER XVI

THE TRUE FUNCTIONS OF A "HOLDING COMPANY"

THE cases I have cited are mere types; they have been repeated many times and subjected to some variations to suit different conditions, but the fundamental principle has remained the same. Always there has been an increase of the load of capitalization under which the enterprise lagged and staggered, and always a part of the securities thus issued, or a part of the money they represented, mysteriously disappeared. The farmer's boy, in the old story, observed that the miller's hogs were very fat. You may notice, similarly, that the syndicate gentlemen have grown very rich.

Even in this brief outline of a long and very intricate story I ought to mention two matters that stand out conspicuously in the succession of questionable transactions.

Probably no other corporation in this or any other country has ever operated under so many different names. To follow the concern through its list of designations from the old Broadway & Seventh Avenue, the names of different subsidiary companies that were made to do duty for the whole, the Metropolitan Street-Railway Company, Metropolitan Traction Company, Metropolitan Securities Company, Interurban Street-Railway Company, New York City Railway Company, the Interborough-Metropolitan Company, and the rest, would be an unprofitable task; but I desire to note one use that has been made of this fugitive and evanescent nomenclature:

The Metropolitan Street-Railway Company was organized under the laws of the State of New York. The Metropolitan Traction Company was organized under the laws of the State of New Jersey. These companies were coexistent, had the same amount of capital stock, the same ostensible purposes, the same management; but the Metropolitan Traction Company, being a New Jersey corporation, was not obliged to make public report of its transactions. When, therefore, the syndicate bought a branch line for $100,000 and sold it for $1,000,000, it always sold to the Metropolitan Traction Company of New Jersey (where the record of the affair was lost), and the Metropolitan

Traction Company of New Jersey sold to the Metropolitan Street-Railway Company of New York, and back of this transaction no investigation could go, because it was a transaction between corporations of different States, and under our wise system this protection to dishonest corporations is absolute and perfect. That little fact explains why most of such corporations doing business in the State of New York are incorporated in New Jersey. The New York courts can have almost no control over them, there is no reason why the New Jersey courts should interfere with them, and thus, to all intents and purposes, they are independent of and superior to the law of any State.

The Metropolitan Traction Company of New Jersey seems also to have had another function in concealing the disappearance of moneys mysteriously missing from the Metropolitan Street-Railway Company of New York. Thus when, in 1898, the Metropolitan Street-Railway Company issued $15,000,000 of additional stock, $6,000,000 thereof, it will be remembered, was to redeem outstanding debenture certificates. These debenture certificates were issued in October, 1897, to pay for property purchased from the Metropolitan Traction Company.

In September, 1896, the Metropolitan Street-Railway Company had issued, and delivered to the Metropolitan Traction Company, $13,500,000 of stock, in payment of other properties and securities purchased from that company. That is all the information made public in regard to these transactions. What were the properties and securities thus acquired? Nobody knows. The items go down in the books, the totals appear in the reports, there is no explanation of the entries, and the properties and securities are left to public surmise. All we know is that the Metropolitan Traction Company, owned by the syndicate, had no legitimate function in the operating of the street-railroad system of New York, that it was used as a clearing-house for the secret deals of the syndicate, and that here in these two items a total of $19,500,000 of the stockholders' money was paid to it on a bald entry.

The other matter I should tell relates to the Third Avenue Company, which for many years had remained independent and outside of the syndicate's control. In the early part of 1900 the syndicate saw that the time had come when it might possess this long-coveted property. The Third Avenue owned or controlled a very great trackage, and had been one of the most staid and powerful corporations of the city.   It had changed its motive power, about 1892, from horse to cable, and five or six years later it changed again from cable to the underground electric trolley.   This latter change, by the way, embraces what is to this day one of the business mysteries of New York.   From time to time there were printed in the newspapers hints of a remarkable state of affairs concealed in the huge work of reconstruction, but no one has ever been able to lay hands upon all the threads of the story. It seems certain that the work was enormously and extravagantly expensive—much more expensive than had been planned, and that because of this expense the price of Third Avenue stock fell rapidly in the market, assisted by recurrent reports of the increasing liabilities.   More than this, there appears reason to believe in some malign interference with the operations and welfare of the road.   But beyond these deductions there are only the vaguest surmises as to what actually occurred.

The management of the Third Avenue Company was no longer strong.   Mr. Henry Hart, who had been for years the captain of the enterprise, was growing old and feeble, and the younger hands on the wheel seemed to steer but badly.   Observant persons saw that the ship was sailing a singularly

erratic and perilous course. In these conditions
the price of the stock continued to sag. In two
or three years it had fallen from 232 to 120, and at
that point the syndicate thought it might safely begin to operate. A terrific bear raid was started
against the stock, an assault most cleverly planned
and carefully executed, the newspapers being adroitly tricked into helping. It drove the price from
120 down to 45, at which figure the syndicate
quietly loaded up until it had secured control. By
a device quite familiar in such operations, the syndicate gentlemen had bought while they pretended
to sell, and thus had kept the price down to the
level whither they had forced it. Whereupon they
effected the lease to the Metropolitan of the Third
Avenue and all its allied lines, and the passing into
their hands of practically the entire street-railroad
system of Manhattan and the Bronx.

To pay the floating debt of the Third Avenue
Company and to provide for change of motive power on some of its allied lines, there were now issued
$35,000,000 of Third Avenue bonds—naturally;
consolidation and reorganization have always been
the occasion of more water on the flooded lands.
The floating indebtedness of the company was $22,-
000,000. This left $13,000,000 for the change

of motive power. So far the motive power has
been changed on one and one-quarter miles of the
allied lines, at an actual cost of possibly $400,000.
But the remainder, $12,600,000, seems to have dis-
appeared.

Who got the money?

There is no escape from the conclusion that while
all these things were going on, the enterprise was
steadily plunging down the road to insolvency, and
that the men on the inside knew it while they continued to increase the ruinous load of securities.
For at least the last seven years of its existence
the dividends paid by the Metropolitan must have
been unearned. We are now all accustomed more
or less to exhibitions of cold callousness on the part
of corporation managers, but I doubt if we have
known any such exhibitions as those of the Metropolitan management.

For instance, in 1898 the management decided
to increase the annual dividend from 5 per cent.
to 7 per cent. It is now quite apparent that even
at that time the 5 per cent. dividends were not
earned, but were being paid out of the vital resources of the concern, and this fact must have been
familiar to the men on the inside. Nevertheless,
they announced a dividend of 7 per cent. At this,

of course, the price of Metropolitan stock sailed upward until it reached 269. At this point the men on the inside released a large part of their holdings, and reaped their great profits on the rise they had thus forced. It seems to me that these records do not contain anything more extraordinary than the forced advance to 269 of the stock of a practically bankrupt institution, nor have I ever heard of a hardihood more colossal than that of the men that put it up, knowing full well the real nature of the securities they were juggling, and knowing, also, that they themselves were responsible for the practical ruin of the enterprise.

The whole thing was utterly impossible; any inspection of the existing conditions would have shown that it was impossible. The lease of the Third Avenue line alone was made on terms that would have bankrupted a road far more profitable. The Third Avenue had been a safely managed and solid concern. From the time of its lease to the Metropolitan it began to lose more than $1,000 a day. The dividends guaranteed on the Third Avenue stock when the lease was made were beyond the earning capacity of the road, and every person that knew anything about the street railroad business must from the start have known this also.

Why, then, was such a lease made?

It was made because the insiders had depressed the price of Third Avenue stock to 45 or thereabouts, at which price they had bought heavily until they secured control. With control, they made this impossible lease. With the news of the lease uprose the price of Third Avenue, as well as the price of all the Metropolitan stocks, and from these advances were made millions of profits for the insiders.

Since the lease the floating indebtedness of the Third Avenue Railroad has been enormously increased: the road has issued $1,943,000 of new bonds, and it has lost from its operations about $1,000,000 a year. It has borne, meantime, the burden of $8,000,000 of guaranteed dividends, which, according to the terms of the lease, were to be increased with succeeding years. From conditions like these what in the world could come upon that property but a smash? Thus an enterprise once exceptionally solid and profitable has become a piece of financial wreckage. A separate receivership and the practical obliteration of the stock are threatened, all because the inside has been scooped from the concern.

Who got the money?

Two years later the whole outfit, Metropolitan, Third Avenue, and everything else, was leased to a new company called the Interurban Street-Railway Company. In all these operations the lease is a great matter. It covers up a deal of rottenness, and it once more strikes the rock whence flow the unfailing streams of water wherewith fainting finance is revived. It was so in this case. The Metropolitan then owed $11,000,000, a condition no longer to be concealed; hence the handy lease, more water, more tribute from the public.

According to the statement of President Vreeland, this indebtedness had been incurred in the purchase of Third Avenue stock, and one of the reasons given for the new lease was that funds might be provided for the payment of this indebtedness.

The facts were that the purchase of Third Avenue stock had cost $6,400,000, not $11,000,000, and that even this $6,400,000 had long before been paid. For in 1901 the Metropolitan had issued $7,000,000 of new stock for this purpose, and the stock (thanks to an impressionable public) had been sold at a premium, so that it had realized $10,500,-

ooo, instead of $7,000,000, and the $6,400,000 had been paid off, leaving a handsome balance.

How, then, could there be an indebtedness of $11,000,000 "incurred in the purchase of Third Avenue stock"?

The company's quarterly balance-sheets, filed with the State Railroad Commissioners, sufficiently established the startling discrepancy. Kuhn, Loeb & Co. were then holding about $6,000,000 of the Metropolitan Securities Company stock. The attention of Mr. Jacob Schiff, a member of the firm, was called to the difference between the statement of President Vreeland and the facts as disclosed by the balance-sheets. Mr. Schiff went at once to Mr. Ryan and made a peremptory demand that his firm be instantly relieved of the $6,000,000 of Metropolitan Securities stock. Mr. Ryan lost no time in complying with the demand. Why, one person can guess as well as another. But he certainly complied, and on the spot.

Four years ago Mr. James W. Osborne publicly offered to prove in any court of law that there had been taken from the Metropolitan by the men on the inside not less than $30,000,000. No opportunity was ever given to him to make good his assertion. His challenge was never accepted. But it may be interesting now to recall his offer and to observe at the same time this table of the sums that have disappeared in the various Metropolitan transactions:

Houston Street bonds.........................	$6,000,000.00
"New Construction" Report of 1901............	6,438,541.29
"Leased Line Betterments" Report of 1902......	11,014,730.70
"Track and Roadway Construction" Report of 1902	3,500,000.00
Change of Motive Power, General Report of 1902.	6,000,000.00
Thirty-fourth Street change motive power......	700,000.00
Central Park, North & East River change motive power....................................	1,500,000.00
Twenty-third Street change motive power.......	1,400,000.00
Second Avenue change motive power...........	2,396,218.55
Third Avenue bonds...........................	12,600,000.00
Total	$51,549,490.54

So this is the reason why the Metropolitan with its enormous revenues, its almost unequaled business, its increased receipts and diminished expenses, has gone into the hands of receivers. It is the reason why, when the receivers took possession, they found the entire property in a decayed and dilapidated condition. It is the reason why there were not enough closed cars to equip the road for cold weather. It is the reason why the company operated fewer cars in 1906 than it operated in 1905 and into them crowded, jammed, and mashed a

greater number of people.   It explains why in the
rush hours two-thirds of the passengers are obliged
to hang to straps.   It explains what becomes of
three cents out of every five cents paid for fare.

The enterprise has been monstrously overloaded
with capitalization until it has sunk; a great part
of its securities have disappeared; upon the whole
mass the public is paying the huge interest charges;
for the sake of the fortunes drawn from these ma-
nipulations the public must endure the pains of an
inadequate and uncomfortable service.

If it is necessary that these gentlemen should have
It, should we not fare better if we gave them their
huge fortunes direct from the national treasury and
hired them to keep their hands off us and our affairs?

CHAPTER XVII

THE BRUNT OF THE BURDEN

WHENEVER there is unpleasant comment about these achievements in finance the financiers invariably take refuge behind a denunciation of "muckraking" as a menace to the business stability of the country.

In other words here is shown for us another glimpse of that beautiful inverted pyramid about which we mused as we moved up the avenue of palaces at the outset of these chronicles. The palace-dwellers not only furnish employment for the 1,500,000 of the poor and the 2,000,000 of the very poor, but they furnish prosperity for all the country. If you attack them you are assailing the very foundation stone of national commerce.

Nor can this be a mere jest or pleasantry, as you may see for yourself. It was the New York Public Service Commission that brought forth the testimony of Anthony N. Brady concerning the Wall and Cortland Street ferries deal. When that story was laid bare by the persistent questioning of the commission's counsel, there arose a loud wail of anguish from some of our best citizens and a demand that the investigation take another line. Because if the commission persisted in unearthing these frauds business confidence and business stability would be destroyed and there was no telling whither the disaster might run nor what might be its consequences.

So if these gentlemen that do these things are right, the true basis of modern business is not integrity (as the foolish have supposed), but the privilege to break the law and be immune from punishment; and the most important thing for us all is that there should be water-built palaces and unlimited loot.

But suppose we look a little further. Is it really necessary that we should endure these things lest we plunge down the pit of business disaster?

I know a man, a typical American flat-dweller, a typical example among the 1,500,000, a good example of those that labor and dream of advancement and incentive. A good man, he has not a vice nor an expensive habit; an industrious man, he has toiled faithfully for twenty years in one employment; an intelligent man, thoughtful, well-read, well-educated. He has a little family; there are four in his flat. His two ambitions have been to lay by for his family and to win advancement in his work. By personal economies and self-denials he put aside a few dollars month by month from the close margin of his salary. He kept his nest egg in a savings bank. He watched it grow slowly year by year. It was not much, but it was something. He felt that with more economies and self-denials it would some day be almost a competence.

He watched things and waited. He saw the Metropolitan taking shape. He saw it absorbing one property after another. The newspapers that he read taught him that these consolidations always effected economies in operations and enhanced the profits. New York was growing rapidly. Every year the Metropolitan carried more people; he was sure that every year it would contrive to carry still more people. It was a solid, permanent institution, having at its head some of our very best citizens and most respected leaders in the great business world.

It looked good to him.

He talked with men whose business it is to know the utmost shred of truth about investments. Invariably they said that Metropolitan was a grand

thing. How could it be otherwise? Look at the
men at the head of it. Look at its business. Look
at its advantages. Had not the people conferred
upon it free of charge the exclusive possession of
their best streets? Did it not have a franchise in
Broadway for 999 years? Did it not have many
other franchises safeguarding it for generations to
come? Safe! What could be safer?

He talked also with other wise men of affairs,
with bankers and solid business men, and they as-
sured him that here he could incur no risk. Such
a business! Such a daily harvest of profits! Such
a solid enterprise! Who could imagine a disaster
befalling it?

He read what in the financial columns seemed
to bear on the enterprise; he meditated long and
consulted well. And then he drew out his little savings and bought stock of the Metropolitan Street
Railway Company.

For five years it paid 5 or 7 per cent. dividends
and the man often thought how wise he was to
invest his savings in it.

It will not pay any more dividends of 7 or
any other per cent. To all practical intents and
purposes it is worth to-day the paper it is printed
on and no more. It never will be worth any more.

The man's savings have been swept out of existence in the fall of the looted structure and he will not be able to extract a cent from the ruins.

That is one case I know of. A sufferer recounting in the *Cosmopolitan Magazine* for January, 1908, his own similar experience, assures us of another. Without question there must be thousands more.

Real prosperity is built not upon unlimited opportunity to loot, but upon the purchasing power of large masses of people. How about that purchasing power when such institutions as this are operating to sweep away savings? How about the inverted pyramid? How about the support of the 1,500,000 and the 2,000,000 by the 10,000?

Also, how about one other thing? How about opportunity in this blessed land? This flat-dweller is continually told that if he will but try he can scale the precipitous path that leads to competence. So he tries, after the manner approved by all the sage moralists of optimism. He is thrifty, economical, self-denying, sober, upright, industrious, as these eminent authorities tell him he should be. He looks up from the ledge where he clings with his $1,639 of total possessions and he is determined to rise as becomes a free and independent Ameri-

can.   He reads the story of this man and that, great
in the dazzling way of finance.   He walks up the
avenue and sees the beautiful palaces, and the sight
inspires him with the hope that if he cannot have
a palace he can at least move a little from that
ledge where he stands with the 1,500,000.

So he invests his little savings wrenched by sheer
self-denial these years upon years from his toiling
life.   He invests them with the captains of industry
and the captains of industry scoop in his money and
cast him back upon his ledge.   And on this ledge
you may be sure he will stay the rest of his life.

Other things would combine to keep him there
if he had never lost a dollar in the Metropolitan,
nor in any other scheme of the palace-dwellers.   He
observes that year by year it costs him more to live,
that his butcher bills grow and his grocer bills increase and his clothes cost more and the rent of the
flat goes up, as year by year a larger proportion of
the products of industry are by means of the
watered stock and the fraudulent bond diverted to
the clutches of the palace-dwellers.

But he finds that his income does not keep pace
with this enforced increase of expenditures.

For he must pay for these new Chicago & Alton
bonds, every one of them; he must pay for these

amazing feats in financial legerdemain; he must
pay for the overcapitalized railroads and the loot-
ing express companies and all the rest of the grand
old game.

That being the case—what chance has he?

CHAPTER XVIII

THE EXPERIENCES OF A WITNESS

As a general rule the personal side of these matters is not worth going into. The issue is not one of individuals, but of principles. We do not generally care very much who attacks wrong if it but be attacked. And we do not care at all what may have been his particular experiences in the fight; the cause is beyond all that. But here is a story of such experiences that I wish to relate in full because it has an application too broad and too pertinent to be overlooked and because it reveals something of the extraordinary power to which corporations may attain before we are aware.

The man that turned up the whole story of the Metropolitan manipulation is Col. William N. Amory of New York City. His investigations conducted at his own expense paved the way to all we know of these performances in profits.

Col. Amory is an experienced and expert street

railroad executive. He was for a time Secretary of the old Third Avenue Railroad Company. He understands the mystery behind which is cloaked the real significance of railroad reports; he knows how to analyze these statements and pluck out their true meaning.

In 1902 Col. Amory was asked by the district attorney of New York to furnish some information and memoranda concerning the condition and methods of the Metropolitan, which were then beginning to attract much attention. He went to work on the company's reports. He had long regarded these documents as untrustworthy; he soon discovered evidence that the wrong-doing had far exceeded his suspicions.

Then he began to make his discoveries public and to draw to them the attention of the district attorney.

Now, the men that in these ways make these huge fortunes are not particularly sensitive to public opinion, but they do hate the idea of going before a district attorney.

The first thing they had to do was to discredit Col. Amory. So they resorted to the weapons most commonly used against men that disturb privilege and attack vested interests. They said he was a liar and they tried to discover or manufacture a flaw in his private character.

First they issued a statement branding all his revelations as utterly false and libelous and declaring an intention to punish him to the fullest extent of the law. This was duly and fully circulated. Then through their press agents they ridiculed him, and discovered and magnified faults in his accusations, and ignored the real point of his revelations; and by these means they actually created in the community a feeling that Col. Amory was untrustworthy and that his attacks on the Metropolitan were instigated by personal malice and were untrue, a conviction furthered by the refusal of the district attorney to take up the charges that Col. Amory had filed with him. One of the officers of the Metropolitan, overstepping once the bounds of discretion usually pursued by men of his class, made an overt statement. He said that Col. Amory was a stock-jobber (as well as a liar) and that his attacks on the Metropolitan had been made to rig the stock market and for the purpose of being bought off. Col. Amory promptly sued this person for libel; which had the effect of discouraging any further comments of a public nature. But the adroit secret campaign went on and Col.

Amory was soon generally disbelieved and disliked. Business men did not care to have anything to do with him; he found the usual avenues of profitable business closed to him.

Meantime a very singular campaign had been going on against his personal character. He was watched and followed day and night by detectives. A house near his was rented as headquarters for the watchers. Every person that called at Col. Amory's home was followed when he left and an attempt was made to learn his business. Members of the family were kept under surveillance whenever they went out. Col. Amory's servants were bribed and his telephone wire was tapped. Every telegram delivered at his house bore evidence that it had been opened and read.

Presently he discovered that his mail was being tampered with and in a way that seemed to leave no doubt of collusion on the part of some person in the post-office service.

Now, this is a very remarkable story and reads like a page of improbable fiction, and yet it is all serious fact and these things really happened in the city of New York and in these days of ours—as you shall see.

Col. Amory's personal attorney was William R.

Brinkerhoff, No. 68 William Street. On the morning of December 4, 1903, Mr. Brinkerhoff received at his office in the usual way a letter addressed in his care to Col. Amory. This letter came from Washington, being postmarked "Washington, D. C., Dec. 3, 1903."

Mr. Brinkerhoff put the letter into an envelope of his own, sealed it and addressed it to Col. Amory at his residence.

This package was delivered at Col. Amory's residence at 5 o'clock that afternoon. Col. Amory opened it and found inside nothing but a sheet of white paper.

Later the postman delivered at Col. Amory's house a plain envelope addressed to Mrs. Amory. When this was opened it was found to contain the letter that had been received at Mr. Brinkerhoff's office for Col. Amory. But that letter had been opened and was now outside of its original envelope —which was also enclosed. It was a letter from a woman.

In the next few days Mrs. Amory received anonymous letters the plain purpose of which was to induce her to proceed against her husband for infidelity, for they offered to supply her with evidence, or as the letter said "to produce the girl at the slightest sign from you." Another letter made a direct reference to the communication that Mr. Brinkerhoff had forwarded and to its contents. Those annoyances continued, while the close watch kept upon Mrs. Amory's movements justified the belief that she was expected to consult a lawyer with intent to secure a divorce. On May 4th Mrs. Amory received an exact duplicate of the Washington letter of December 3d, even the cancellation mark on the postage stamp being most cleverly imitated in india-ink. Accompanying this was a letter signed "M. R.," urging Mrs. Amory to investigate her husband's actions.

Col. Amory now made a series of tests to determine absolutely whether the mails were being tampered with. He found that seals were no protection to letters addressed to him and that even registered letters were opened en route. He also discovered that whenever he or one of his family mailed a letter in a street letter box some one immediately appeared and put into the box a yellow envelope of a peculiar design. He learned from a post-office inspector to whom he complained of these things that post-office detectives used these yellow envelopes to indicate the posting of a letter by a suspected person that they were watching.

Hence it was obvious that these envelopes were now being used to indicate to someone in the postal service the position of a letter from Col. Amory.

These annoyances continued about two years. When Col. Amory published an account of them the public received the story with utter incredulity. What! Detectives and spies opening letters and tampering with the mails? In this day? Impossible! The man must be mad or dreaming. So people said, and Col. Amory suffered still further in his standing and his charges against the Metropolitan seemed lighter than ever.

And yet in both matters he was destined to have a signal vindication. When the Public Service Commission took up the testimony of Brady concerning the Wall and Cortland Street ferries line, it struck upon the identical thing that Col. Amory had from the first insisted was the practice of the Metropolitan insiders and found ample reason to believe that all his statements pertaining thereto were correct. And a little later the man that in the Metropolitan service has charge of such pleasant matters admitted on the stand that Col. Amory's story about the detectives was equally correct.

For this work the funds belonging to the Metropolitan stockholders had been used. The cost

was charged to the same account as the expenses of
the Civic Federation's Committee, which went
abroad (at the instigation of the public utility corporations) and reported Municipal Ownership in
Europe to be a failure.

Perhaps the defrauded stockholder that now con-
templates the destruction of his holdings under the
reorganization that will follow the receivership
may be consoled to learn thus definitely what has
become of a part of his money.

As to the tampering with the mails and the apparent collusion in the post-office service, I do not
pretend to know the exact methods by which such
things can be brought about. Only I do know that
this is not the first time persons concerned in these
events have been able to exert some influence over
the operations of Government.

To see how fortunate they have been in this regard it is only necessary to revert for a moment to
the story of the State Trust Company.

CHAPTER XIX

SIDE-LIGHTS ON CIVILIZATION IN A GREAT CITY

OUT West, and in other regions to which we in the metropolis are apt to refer at times with a fat and complacent superiority, a street-car drawn with horses has long been a curiosity for antiquarians, a strange relic of dead ages, a reminiscence of the times before electricity was heard of, when men lived in sod houses and wore coonskin shirts.

Is it not strange then that in New York City there should still be miles upon miles of street-railroad operated exactly as street-railroads were operated sixty years ago and with about the same cars —and horses? Yet such is the fact. The people of a thousand small towns on the prairies or in the mountains can ride in swiftly moving trolley-cars; the people of a large part of New York City are condemned to antique rattle-traps of our great-grandfathers. Of the street-railroad mileage that in the State of New York is still operated with horse-power about ninety per cent. lies in the city the largest and haughtiest on this continent and almost the largest in the world.

For this extraordinary fact try to imagine if you can one other reason except that the money that should have gone to modernizing these railroads has been swallowed up in interest charges and dividends on watered stocks and bonds; try to imagine, if you can, one other reason why the public must bear the burden of this outworn and inadequate equipment.

One of these New York City lines that still cling to the methods of medievalism is the line that runs eastward in Twenty-eighth Street and westward in Twenty-ninth, and standing at the corner of Madison Avenue and Twenty-eighth Street one afternoon last winter this archaic relic afforded me a very strange and I think an instructive spectacle.

There was beginning a howling blizzard from the northwest. Very likely you know or can imagine how the wind tears through the east and west streets when that kind of affliction descends upon us. The snow drove heavily and as if shot from a gun. There came along the street a perfect old Noah's ark of a car, battered, scratched, visibly shaking as if with palsy, and crowded to the last inch of its capacity. Men and women stood in the aisle crushed so tightly one marveled they could breathe, the platforms were full, men stood upon the steps. At the back of and outside the rear platform ran a little rail crosswise of the car and upon this stood a crowd of shivering male bipeds, clinging desperately with hands and feet. A more forlorn and wretched lot I have never seen. The wind hurled the snow into the faces and ears and down the necks of the people on the platform, who were so closely wedged together they could lift no hand to wipe away the chilly slush. Icy drops fell from the eaves of the roof upon them; the wind buffeted them cruelly. In front two weary and dispirited horses tugged at the monstrous load, and upon the worn-out track the car lurched and shook and rumbled.

At Madison Avenue two or three women and a man had been standing in the whirling snow waiting for this car. They signaled for it to stop. The driver as he went by shot out a lip at them and grinned expressively. He did not stop. The women and the man went back in silence to the sidewalk and resumed their waiting in the whirling snow. They were New Yorkers; they were trained to this sort of thing.*

One of the women carried a great bundle; somebody's washing, I suppose. Her hands were bare and with the cold had turned a livid blue. She shifted her bundle and tried in her shawl to warm the disengaged hand. She was quite elderly; the snow that clung to her hair seemed of the same color. She stamped her feet on the ground to keep them from freezing. A closed automobile whizzed by filled with comfortable people. The old woman leaped back that the machine should not run over her half-frozen feet. The chauffeur looked down and laughed.

When I returned to my room I picked up a defense (written by an eminent authority) of the practice of stock-watering. Somehow the arguments did not ring very true. I kept on seeing that car and that old woman.

But let us be perfectly fair. This is the price of stock-watering, but the men that water the stocks are not without a semblance of reason and plausibility on their side, nor is there one thing in all the

---

*A very able Kansas City editor, writing once about such matters, termed us "the most thoroughly subjugated people on earth." There are times and occasions when, to the observer, that phrase will recur as eminently apt and just.

operations we have described for which a pretext has not been found both in economics and in morals. So strange are the operations of the human mind that without a doubt the practitioners of these methods (and many other persons) have long ago persuaded themselves that to make money in these ways is fair and right and ought not to be attacked lest the foundations of business stability be threatened. And to the speculative philosopher I suppose there is no other phase of the whole subject so interesting as this.

It is time, then, to hear the other side of these matters. What is it that, being urged in defense of these corporations, enables the men that profit by them to proceed composedly upon their way and many other men to hesitate in their judgment?

Well, it is this—and if I do not state the argument with perfect fairness I hope to be corrected.

The practice of overcapitalization, or, in a common phrase, of stock-watering, is defended on two grounds:

First, any enterprise may legitimately, justly, and properly be capitalized to the full extent of its earning power. For instance, let us suppose a commercial or manufacturing enterprise with a capital of $100,000. It grows in prosperity until it is making, let us say, $25,000 a year. If it were to be sold no man in his senses would argue that it should be sold for $100,000. At the rates for money current until within a few months an enterprise earning $25,000 a year might justly be held to be worth $400,000. Now, if its value to sell is $400,000 no one can find fault if it be capitalized at $400,000, and if the owners by increasing its capital reap in that way the legitimate profit of the increased business, which, in their opinion doubtless, their own ability, energy, and foresight have created, to do so is their legal right. In the same way a railroad company, a traction company, or a gas company, making profits in excess of the prevailing rate of interest, is entitled to increase its capital to a point where the interest rate it earns shall be on a plane with current average rates.

Second, these increases in capital in no way affect the public and are not the public's concern.

So men say. But how does this matter really stand?

The argument about the legitimacy of capitalizing the earning power takes no account of the vicissitudes of business conditions, and that is the very point that in the case of public utilities like transportation and lighting is of supreme impor-

tance. Your $100,000 enterprise that earns $25,-
000 this year may next year earn only $5,000 or it
may earn nothing at all. With profits of $5,000
it can pay dividends on a capital of $100,000; it
can pay none on a capital of $400,000. Suppose,
then, the public to have purchased the additional
issue of stock (when the capital was increased from
$100,000 to $400,000) in the expectation of a
$25,000 profit. If there be no dividends forth-
coming the value of that stock declines, and there
are not only losses and embarrassments to the holders, but there has been loosed a tremendous power
to destroy confidence, to upset business, and to
cause a row of additional losses like a row of falling bricks.

Because the stock has been deposited with the
banks as collateral and as the price of it falls the
banks throw it upon a falling market or demand
further collateral to protect their loans. So that
daily over our heads hangs this sword of the unsafe
loan collateral—so long as we have watered stocks.

Moreover, while all this is bad enough in the
case of an enterprise of a private nature (an enterprise with which the public can deal or not deal
as it chooses), there are in the case of a public utility like a railroad or a street-car line many evils in-

finitely worse. If the managers of a private enterprise attempt, by increasing prices, or by impairing service, to make up a deficit in profits, the public can usually avoid the imposition by avoiding the product of that enterprise. But it has no such chance in the case of a public utility. There is but the one gas company; the public must at the price demanded take the gas or go without. There is but one traction company; the public must submit to the overcrowding or walk.

Again, in the case of the public utility the increase of the capital is almost invariably made in advance of the increase of business, so that what is capitalized is not what the enterprise has earned, but what it can be twisted, forced, and driven into earning. And these processes of forced earnings in the end resolve themselves into merely two propositions:

Either the charges that the public must pay are increased;

Or the service that the public must endure is impaired.

No human ingenuity has ever been able to devise any other way of providing these forced profits.

Sometimes the additional stock or additional bonds that represent the "capitalized earning power" are sold for cash; sometimes they become the private property of the fortunate gentlemen thus possessed of the power to make something out of nothing. Cases are recorded in which the cash obtained from the additional securities loaded upon the public's broad back has been used to improve or maintain the property; very much oftener it is used for no such purpose, but only to acquire, by the issue of excessive capitalization, the possession of other properties already excessively capitalized. But in practically every case a radical improvement of the property is absolutely essential for the welfare and safety of the public, and the money used to pay the interest on the new bonds or the dividends on the new stock is really dug bodily out of the physical condition of the property.

After us the deluge.

You can see at a glance how true this is in the conspicuous instances of the steam-railroads of the country and the traction systems of the cities.

We have now about 218,000 miles of steam-railroad of which only 15,000 miles are double-tracked. Practically the entire mileage should be double-tracked, not only for public safety, but to carry the traffic.

If there were no stock-watering there need be no

single-tracked railroads. The money that normally would have been used for double-tracking has gone for dividends on the watered stock.

We have on our steam-railroads thousands of grade-crossings (a very barbarous and stupid device) by means of which every year hundreds of persons needlessly lose their lives.

If there were no stock-watering there need be no grade-crossings. The money that normally would have been used to abolish these death-traps has gone for dividends on the watered stock.

In the case of the street railroads the vile overcrowding, the strap-hanging, the monstrous discomfort, the infrequent cars, the bad tracks, the wretched conveniences, are merely products of stock-watering.

The money that normally would have gone into adequate equipment has gone for dividends on watered stock.

In the case of the gas companies good gas can be made and sold profitably at fifty cents a thousand feet. We pay, in the majority of cases, $1 or more, and usually get poor gas even at that price.

The odd fifty cents is for dividends on watered stock and excessive bonds.

To illustrate these matters with an applicable incident, several of the Western States have lately passed laws reducing the limit of passenger fares and fixing it in some cases at two cents a mile. An eminent railroad magnate recently returning from his annual vacation in Europe was quoted by newspapers as denouncing this legislation and declaring that if it were not stopped railroads in his control would be driven to withdraw practically from the passenger business and to restrict their energies to the transporting of freight.

It is easily demonstrated that if the stocks of these railroads had never been watered, if, in other words, this mythical earning power had never been capitalized, they could carry passengers at one cent a mile and make much money.

Hence the difference between one cent and three cents, which the railroad magnate thinks should be the rate, is the tax that the public would pay for the existence of the water.

Hence, also, it is solely on account of this water that the railroad magnate threatens us with the loss of transportation facilities.

But what under the sun do we get for our two cents contributed in this cause? What possible good results to us? We pay them, that is certain enough, year in and year out, but what do we get for them? On this point I should love to be instructed. So far I have been unable to learn of any advantage accruing to the public except a view of the exteriors of some of the palaces erected from this water. I think we have never been called an architectural people, but even if we were this privilege, at the price, would seem an over-rated pleasure.

And there is no available refuge in the specious fallacy to the effect that we need not worry about these accumulations, because the money won by these methods is not hoarded, but returned to circulation and the public gets it again. If there were anything in that we should need no laws against burglary, for the burglar does not hoard his gains either. It is quite true that Mr. Rockefeller, for example, does not dig holes in his cellar and hide his gold therein. It is quite true that with the enormous profits he gathers from Standard Oil he buys a gas company and with the profits from the gas-works he buys a trolley-line, and so on. It is also true that gas-works and trolley-line must employ men and pay wages. But the control of the enterprise remains in Mr. Rockefeller's hands; the distribution of the earnings of the enterprise, which was unfair in the beginning, is made still more unfair because he secures for himself a steadily increasing percentage; and the money that he thus gathers under his own control ceases to be any incentive to the endeavors of other men. Above all, as fast as he uses his augmenting profits to purchase additional enterprises he closes with each acquisition another avenue of opportunity and moves us all still farther toward the day that threatens us when we shall be nothing but a nation of hired men and there will be not even a pretense of the old American freedom of opportunity.

So this is the prospect that opens upon the flat-dweller with his $1,639 of total possessions as he looks upward along the track by which men used to climb out of poverty. It has narrowed now to a practically impassable trail; pretty soon it promises to disappear altogether, and he will then be like a man born in India, inexorably fated all his living days to the one station, the one caste, the one monotonous employment.

And if this seems uncheerful for him, how do you think the segregation of the country's available resources affects the men below, men among the 1,500,000 of the poor and the 2,000,000 of the very poor? The dismal and dingy hives in Attorney Street look more forlorn than ever before these certain facts, those dreary regions wherein the people buy coal at the rate of $16 a ton and are by us plucked similarly for other trifles. Not much cheer in the outlook for them, is there? A kind of invisible tube or suction pump is made into each of these dwellings, and there it goes day after day, pumping up the extra cent pieces for the watered stocks of coal companies and the watered stocks of railroad companies, the watered stocks of gas companies and the watered stocks of street-railroad companies, the watered stocks of flour-mills and the watered stocks of elevators. The cost of living mounts grievously upon the inhabitants, we all know that, and from everything they buy there are taken these tributes for the watered stock.

What do you think of it?

It is the fraudulent stock issue and the unfair stock manipulation that from the fund that should be for all draw the useless and senseless hoards of the few. No other nation on earth has ever tolerated any such machine for the making of billion-ares and paupers. Is there not ground for the suspicion that we have tolerated it long enough?

So it is perfect nonsense to say that the public has no concern in these matters; it has every concern in them. For the sake of the $40,000,000 that Mr. Yerkes (by the methods I have described) extracted from the street railroads of Chicago the community endured for many years the most abominable traction service in this world. The $40,-000,000 would have given the people a good service; the difference between the good service and the bad service inflicted upon them meant a sum of inconvenience, discomfort, suffering, and sometimes of impaired health that is revolting to contemplate. In New York the money represented by the water in the street-railroad system would have provided the city with ample, quick, and comfortable transit in all directions. The issuing of that water means the difference between such transit and the terrible scenes witnessed nightly at the Brooklyn Bridge and in the Subway.

Not only that, but it makes the difference between a normal and an abnormal fare. If there never had been any water in the New York street-railroad system, if the total capital represented nothing but the actual investment, if there had never been any experiments with this devilish "capitalizing of the earning power," the street-railroads of New York could carry passengers for three cents and make money. So that of every five cents paid now on these railroads two cents are paid to support the water and three cents in compensation for the service rendered.

And kindly observe again, if you will, that in all these matters the mass of the people has no choice. To the 10,000 of the very rich and the 500,000 of the rich it makes no difference what may be the condition of the New York transportation system. These have their carriages or their automobiles, or if ever any of them happen to make use of a street-car line the time is the time of the least crowding and the least discomfort.

And again, to these also the extra two cents extracted for water in the street-car stocks and the extra fifty cents extracted for water in the gas stocks are matters of no importance.

To the 1,500,000 of the poor and the 2,000,-000 of the very poor they are matters of great importance.

Take one of those shop-girls going to work early in the morning, coming home after six o'clock at night. It is of very great importance to her that of the $5 or $6 that she earns by a week of toil the street-car company takes twenty-four cents to pay for the water in its stocks. When she has paid her board and put aside something for her clothing, twenty-four cents is to her an important sum. It is of very great importance to her that for every thousand feet of gas consumed where she lives her landlady must pay fifty cents for the water in the gas stocks; the landlady only passes the charge (with interest) to the tenants. It is of very grave importance to this shop-girl that after a day of hard toil at her employment she must stand upon her feet for perhaps an hour and be crushed and crowded and subjected to the grossest indignity in the hideous and unutterable conditions that we tolerate in our public conveyances. It is of very grave importance to her; you cannot easily dodge the conviction, if you stop to think of it, that her physical welfare and the physical welfare of her sisters are of grave importance to the rest of society.

From these burdens thus laid upon her she has no escape. She must do her work, and she cannot walk, for on her earnings she can live only at a great distance from her employment; she must report for duty at eight o'clock, she must remain until five or six, she must travel when the traveling crowd is greatest, when the jostling and jamming are most intolerable. She is, therefore, the bound and helpless victim of this system, and straight from her little earnings and the earnings of her kind comes the enforced tribute that renders possible the "capitalizing of the earning power" and all the other pleasant devices of the high finance.

What do you think of it?

Unless we are to take the position that the public exists solely to be the dumb, blind, patient servitor, to furnish these dividends and to keep still about them, how can we suppose that stock-watering is none of the public's concern?

Yet the whole disastrous business has the warrant of long custom and of our established and most strange tolerance, that is very true. Does any one imagine that there is anything new about these ways of Getting It? They have been followed absolutely by two entire generations of fortune-makers. Twenty-five years ago a certain famous pamphlet essayed to show that up to that time there had been wrongfully taken from the resources of the New York Central something like $30,000,000. Those that profited by these operations in the high finance of that day were the men in control of the property; those that suffered were the stockholders at large and the public. A concise view of similar exploitation in another enterprise may be obtained from Mr. Charles Francis Adams's "A Chapter of Erie." Or the curious

may well be referred to the celebrated case of the
bridge at Albany, which long drew from the stockholders of the road (and from the public) a great
annual tribute for the benefit of one family; or to
the familiar story of the private car lines, which
are only another phase of the same general system; or to the story of the National City Bank
and the Custom House site; or to one thousand
other stories, if you care to look them up, all illus-
trating the one principle of unfair advantage and
of burdens piled upon the shoulders of those least
able to bear burdens.

So now we traverse again the beautiful avenue
by the park, and observe the gleaming palaces, the
rapid automobiles, the happy people. But they
have a different look. Clearly that statement of
gained knowledge that shot across our path in the
beginning of our journeying from Attorney Street
to Fifth Avenue was quite correct. We see now
that the first man did not gain his palace by supplying any demand, nor the second by providing
any mart, nor the third by producing any com-
modity, nor the fourth by transporting any goods
or people. These palaces represent no service
to society, no reward for any one thing bettered, no creation, no development, but only the

means to seize and to retain the resources of the country. Very beautiful are the palaces, grand the glory of the avenue. Reflecting upon the shop-girl standing in the street-car and the part she plays in this magnificence, are we quite sure that these splendors are worth the price?

CHAPTER XX

COPARTNERS IN GUILT

SHALL we say that at the bottom of all these achievements is some flaw in the character of the men that do them, something that sets them apart as monstrous or abnormal?

How absurd that will seem if we do but consider of it impartially! These men are not different from other men; they are not sinners above all the other dwellers in this, our country. What nonsense it would be to choose them from the rest for vicarious sacrifice! Given the opportunities and the power a very large number of us would under the system we have created and after the standard we have set up do exactly what they have done.

If I leave a handful of silver dollars on my doorstep with the sign "Take One" and come back to find them gone I shall be but a figure of mirth if I go about denouncing the persons that have accepted my invitation.

Suppose now in the privacy of our consciences we have a little frank talk with ourselves. What kind of a man is it that, for the last generation at least, we most have honored? The successful man. And what to our minds has invariably and solely constituted success? Piles of dollars. And how have we regulated the fervor of our applause for these men? By the size of their dollar piles. And have we ever stopped to bother very much about the means by which the piles were gathered? Not once that I can remember.

Well—what would you expect?

Let me tell you of two men I happen to know about, and probably they will remind you of a hundred similar men that have crossed your own observation. One by gambling in the necessities of life had accumulated a vast fortune. Sometimes for millions of people he made bread dear and sometimes he made meat dear. He entered into illegal arrangements with railroads. He made illegal combinations with other men in his way of business. Once his firm was discovered to have issued fraudulent warehouse receipts and a scapegoat was put forward to take the heavy blame that there was too much reason to think belonged elsewhere. But the man made money, he made much money, and when he died the newspapers eulogized him and idolized him and from a hundred pulpits resounded fervent praise, for this was the career that to the admiration and edification of young men was held up as the career of a model American.

The other man was a merchant. He paid to his employees a smaller rate of wages than in his town any other merchant paid. He evaded his taxes. He violated city ordinances and a State law. He disregarded a decision of the Supreme Court. He made money and invested in corporations that prospered by breaking the federal statutes. He was a keen bargainer; he gathered a great fortune. But he had no interest in life outside of his steadily increasing hoards, and in the course of a long career he never once manifested the slightest concern about any civic duty. All of his existence and all of his faculties were centered in sordid gain by whatsoever means, although for many years he had possessed wealth immeasurably beyond his utmost needs.

This man died and the newspapers and pulpits uttered of him praise that would have been extravagant for a great philanthropist or public benefactor, hailing him as more truly the model American than the other, even more admirable, even more to be imitated by our youth.

None of us can remember a time when we did not do this sort of thing.

If then it be true that the model American career is one devoted to grabbing money by whatsoever means, how shall we now turn about and condemn the men that have literally accepted our ideal as we have held it up to them? For the great majority of men in this world a moral code is simply the opinions of the men about them. No man can be blamed for desiring and seeking the praise of his fellows. Heretofore we have given our praise to the money-getters. Then shall we profess astonishment that men do extreme things to get money —now that we are all discovering what that means for the rest of us?

Some of us have talked much and written much about retribution for the men that have done these things, bringing the law down upon them or— comical thought!—subjecting them to a "social ostracism," whatever that may be.

How foolish that seems! Come, let us be frank. Who is to blame for all these occurrences? You and I are to blame. We have created and tolerated and enlarged and admired the conditions that

make possible the accumulating of these hoards and
the oppressing of these populations; we have
pointed out to our fellows the Agreeable Formula
and the way to use it; we have responded with our
plaudits and our earnings when use has been made
of it exactly in accordance with our indications.
So long as we leave our dollars on our door-steps
we need not expect to find them there on our return. So long as we give over public utilities to
private greed we should expect to have them used
for the piling up of great fortunes at our expense.

So the next time I see that terribly crowded car
bumping along Twenty-eighth Street, the next time
my ribs are imperiled in the Subway crush, the next
time I hang to a strap in a Broadway car, the next
time I am defrauded on a railroad or a sleeping-
car, I shall, if I am fair and just, utter no com-
plaint against the syndicate, nor revile the traction
management, nor curse the railroad company, but
seek some quiet spot and sedulously kick myself.
For in conjunction with a similar incapacity on the
part of my fellow citizens, my vast inability to
manage my own affairs is responsible for all this;
yes, even for the tortures of the weary shop-girl
standing in the cruelly crowded car, even for the
confiding stockholders that lose their investments,

even for the watered-stock panics that sweep over the country. Elsewhere in the world civilization proceeds without these troubles. What is wrong with us that it is attended by them here?

Where did the gentlemen Get It? They Got It from us and by means of our own witless connivance, brethren. For do you not suppose that if we try we can take those filching fingers from our pockets?

THE END

Confessions of a Muck-Raker

How I Came to Write an Exposé of the
Beef Trust, Instead of an Essay on
the Amphibrach Foot.

LIKE many other Americans, I had long known
in a general way that some of the great corporations of this country were lawless and greedy; but
I did not hold that fact to be any especial concern of mine, and having, for the first time
in my life, a little leisure, I was wholly engrossed
in writing a book (which I knew no one would
ever read) about Algernon Charles Swinburne.
One day, as I was making some musical analyses of
the amphibrach foot, there was brought to me a telegram from my friend Mr. Ridgway, of *Everybody's*, asking me to see J. W. Midgley, in Chicago, and induce him to write "an article on the

basis of his extraordinary testimony." With not the best grace in the world I left the amphibrach foot and started from Evanston (where I was then living) for Chicago. On the way it occurred to me that it might be as well to discover what this "extraordinary testimony" was about. So I bought a newspaper and looked it up.

What I read gave me a new sensation. I knew Mr. Midgley to be of high character and great experience in railroad matters, but it did not seem to me possible that what he was reported to have said could be an accurate representation of an existing condition in any civilized country. He was testifying before the Interstate Commerce Commission concerning what seemed to be a huge commercial tyranny, as arbitrary, as cruel and as oppressive as ever was any satrapy in the Old World. I went to his office and saw him. He took Mr. Ridgway's proposal under consideration. When I left him I did not feel much minded toward the amphibrach foot. I thought I would stroll over to the Interstate Commerce Commission and see if there was any more extraordinary testimony. I could take up the amphibrach foot later.

There was a man on the stand, testifying, a clean-cut, blue-eyed, honest-faced Welshman, and he was telling how, because he had ventured to oppose this commercial tyranny, he had been pursued and threatened and persecuted and nearly ruined. Another man came to the stand and told how a farmer in Southern Illinois had toiled all summer over a little patch of ground, only to find when he had sent his produce to market that this commercial tyranny had levied toll upon it until he not only received nothing, but owed on his shipments. And other witnesses told other stories of hardship and injustice at the hands of this same power; and all these stories centered about the operating of a monopoly of refrigerator cars owned or controlled by the Beef Trust, and all were statements wholly incompatible with any theory of free government and wholly calculated to start boiling blood in the veins of any American. Two days later, when Mr. Midgley found he had no time to write the article, and Mr. Ridgway wired me if I would write it, I popped back "Yes" before I knew it; and to my infinite dismay as soon as I had time to reflect.

So there I was, plunged with no volition of mine into the fight. I had lived some years in Chicago, but had never been to Packingtown, and, except an olfactory evidence, had no idea where it was. I had to begin at the beginning and learn the ropes, dividing my days between Packingtown and South Water Street, where the produce commission houses were. Soon I discovered that no one article would hold this subject, and before long *Everybody's* had agreed to use a series instead of one paper.

I knew that so soon as one article should appear, information would be hard to get, and I figured that I had about three months for unimpeded investigation. I found, as a matter of fact, that I had not been at work ten days before I was an object of marked suspicion in the Stock Yards region, and soon afterward I was aware that I was under a careful espionage. Presently the sources of information seemed to close against me, and I learned that wherever I went I was followed, that persons to whom I spoke were visited and warned, and it was well understood about the yards that I was a visitor of evil intent and not to be talked with. I had not been at pains to conceal a connection with *Everybody's Magazine*, Mr. Lawson's revelations of "Frenzied Finance" were then appearing in that periodical, and it is evident to me now that my appearance was construed as foreshadowing an attack, though at the time why I should have been so quickly suspected and checkmated was a matter of the greatest perplexity to me.

Meanwhile, although I had secured a working basis of knowledge concerning the business, I lacked innumerable and indispensable details that I could see no way of getting, and my dilemma was greatly aggravated by the discovery that another magazine was working upon the same lines. From this trying position I was now rescued by three circumstances, over none of which had I the least control. The first of these was a very good friend in Packingtown, who undertook, at some risk to himself, to secure every detail about which I was perplexed. For the second, I fell accidentally against one end of a remarkable private quarrel within the ramparts of the Trust, and one party to this quarrel saw an interest in putting me in the way to get inside information. Even at this distance I do not see that I am called upon to be more explicit, but I may say that the row involved one of the most extraordinary stories I have ever known and one still, I believe, wholly buried beneath the records of Packingtown.

The third factor was still more remarkable, and remains to this day a mystery to me. On the publication of the first article I began to receive an immense number of letters, some anonymous and of a disagreeable nature. In the lot there came every day, at exactly the same hour, a brief typewritten, unsigned communication that proved of the greatest possible use to me. There was then in Chicago a certain man that, above all other men, should have had no communication with the managers of the Beef Trust. These letters began by reporting every day the movements of this man, showing that he was frequently in consultation with those managers. Upon this information I put what is called an "operative"; he reported that the information was absolutely correct; but while, day after day, the report of the operative and the report of my unknown correspondent entirely agreed, the operative could never discover that any one else was watching the suspected man. The letters now proceeded to give me a series of invaluable hints as to my investigation. Invariably, after most careful investigation, I found these perfectly correct, and from them I was led to a mass of information far beyond my requirements. The letters continued for some weeks and then stopped as abruptly as they began. I need hardly say that nothing they contained was ever given credence without complete investigation; yet the curious fact is that I never once found them to contain an error. To this day I have not the slightest idea of the identity of my correspondent; but one thing was clear—he was not seeking reward or revenge.

Great efforts were made to discredit the articles when they appeared. A campaign was organized, the advertising agencies were enlisted, and huge advertisements of Trust goods were given to every newspaper that would print an editorial denouncing me. A cry was ingeniously raised that I had slandered the people of Iowa and an impression created that I had said many things I had never said. An officer of the United States Government, who is now president of a Trust bank of Chicago, was induced to write an article refuting my charges, about which he knew nothing. But all these things were mere incidents. The subsequent vindication by the action of the courts and the narrow escape of the Trust gentlemen by the application of the "immunity bath" need not be recounted here.

Thus I began to muck-rake. I have been muck-raking ever since. I hope to keep on muck-raking. I like to muck-rake. No doubt I do it badly, but I like it. It isn't as calm and peaceful a pursuit as analyzing the amphibrach foot, but it seems to have more relation to living men and to be of immeasurably more use. I find that when a man has tried with what little facility he has to do a job of muckraking he can review the day with some satisfaction; because, no matter how ill he has done the work, at least he has been trying to be of some slight use to somebody besides himself. That satisfaction does not pertain to the amphibrach foot.

Charles Edward Russell.

COSIMO is a specialty publisher for independent authors, not-for-profit organizations, and innovative businesses, dedicated to publishing books that inspire, inform, and engage readers around the world.

Our mission is to create a smart and sustainable society by connecting people with valuable ideas. We offer authors and organizations full publishing support, while using the newest technologies to present their works in the most timely and effective way.

COSIMO BOOKS offers fine books that inspire, inform and engage readers on a variety of subjects, including personal development, socially responsible business, economics and public affairs.

COSIMO CLASSICS brings to life unique and rare classics, representing a wide range of subjects that include Business, Economics, History, Personal Development, Philosophy, Religion & Spirituality, and much more!

COSIMO REPORTS publishes reports that affect your world, from global trends to the economy, and from health to geopolitics.

COSIMO B2B offers custom editions for historical societies, museums, companies and other organizations interested in offering classic books to their audiences, customized with their own logo and message. **COSIMO B2B** also offers publishing services to organizations, such as media firms, think tanks, conference organizers and others who could benefit from having their own imprint.

FOR MORE INFORMATION CONTACT US AT
INFO@COSIMOBOOKS.COM

➤ if you are a book lover interested in our current list of titles

➤ if you represent a bookstore, book club, or anyone else interested in special discounts for bulk purchases

➤ if you are an author who wants to get published

➤ if you represent an organization or business seeking to publish books and other publications for your members, donors, or customers.

**COSIMO BOOKS ARE ALWAYS
AVAILABLE AT ONLINE BOOKSTORES**

———— **VISIT COSIMOBOOKS.COM** ————
BE INSPIRED, BE INFORMED

9 781646 798834